From Sinai to Calvary

Condensed Sermons on Salvation Themes

by

Henry Clay Morrison

First Fruits Press
Wilmore, Kentucky
c2015

From Sinai to Calvary: Condensed Sermons on Salvation Themes by
Henry Clay Morrison
First Fruits Press, © 2015
Previously published by the Pentecostal Publishing Company, ©1942

Digital version at
http://place.asburyseminary.edu/firstfruitsheritagematerial/92/

ISBN: 9781621711902 (Print), 9781621711896 (Digital)

First Fruits Press is a digital imprint of the Asbury Theological Seminary, B.L. Fisher Library. Asbury Theological Seminary is the legal owner of the material previously published by the Pentecostal Publishing Co. and reserves the right to release new editions of this material as well as new material produced by Asbury Theological Seminary. Its publications are available for noncommercial and educational uses, such as research, teaching and private study. First Fruits Press has licensed the digital version of this work under the Creative Commons Attribution Noncommercial 3.0 United States License. To view a copy of this license, visit http://creativecommons.org/licenses/by-nc/3.0/us/.

For all other uses, contact First Fruits Press.

Morrison, H. C. (Henry Clay), 1857-1942.
   From Sinai to Calvary : condensed sermons on salvation themes / by H.C. Morrison.
   160 pages ; 21 cm.
   Wilmore, Ky. : First Fruits Press, c2015.
   Reprint. Previously published: Louisville, KY : Pentecostal Publishing Company, ©1942.
   ISBN: 9781621711902 (pbk.)
   1. Salvation -- Sermons. 2. Methodist Church -- Sermons. 3. Evangelistic sermons. 4. Sermons, American. I. Title.
BT753 .M6 2015   252.3

Cover design by Haley Hill

First Fruits Press
The Academic Open Press of Asbury Theological Seminary
204 N. Lexington Ave., Wilmore, KY 40390
859-858-2236
first.fruits@asburyseminary.edu
asbury.to/firstfruits

REV. H. C. MORRISON

FROM SINAI TO CALVARY

CONDENSED SERMONS

ON

SALVATION THEMES

BY

DR. H. C. MORRISON

PENTECOSTAL PUBLISHING COMPANY.
LOUISVILLE, KENTUCKY.

COPYRIGHT, 1942
BY
PENTECOSTAL PUBLISHING COMPANY
LOUISVILLE, KENTUCKY

DEDICATION

To the great Herald Family who have been my inspiration and moral support through the Fifty-Four years of The Herald's history, and the "household of God" who have been won to Christ through my ministry.

INTRODUCTION

In this book, "From Sinai to Calvary," we have the condensed cream from Dr. H. C. Morrison's variety of sermons which he preached throughout the nation and around the world.

In these messages one feels the warm heart and eloquent deliverance of one who was truly a prophet of the Lord, and who was bold to declare that God is able to save *all men* from *all sin*, through the atoning blood of Christ.

The publishing of a book of sermons was one thing I insisted that Dr. Morrison should do, and his friends will be glad to know they can still feast on the soul-stirring messages they have heard in other days, and those who have not heard them, will have the joy of reading them from one, "whom having not seen they love."

Here is a treasure-house full of richest gems of gospel truth that have been the means of the salvation of thousands of souls, and will continue to feed and nourish hungry hearts as they live over again the ministry of this Defender of the glorious truth that, "Without holiness no man shall see the Lord."

May the blessing of the Lord rest upon each one who reads these sermons from the heart and passionate longing of one who now rests from his labors. Our departed Warrior "fought a good fight," and is now enjoying the presence of his Christ whom he preached as an uttermost Savior.

Devotedly Yours,

MRS. H. C. MORRISON.

CONTENTS

CHAPTER PAGE
1. The Value Of A Soul 7
2. The Universal Curse 19
3. Fulness of Redemption 28
4. The Revelation Of The Trinity 36
5. An Uttermost Salvation 42
6. Babes In Christ 49
7. The Carnal Mind and Its Cure........ 57
8. Traits of Carnality 64
9. The Mind of Christ 73
10. Development of Christian Character.... 80
11. God's Plan For A Revival 86
12. The Artillery Of Heaven 101
13. Rejected Light 111
14. Seeking A Bride For Isaac 119
15. The Baptism With The Holy Spirit.....126
16. The Christ Of Prophecy 135
17. National Security 145
18. How To Bring A Sinner To Christ 154
(The last sermon Dr. Morrison preached.)

CHAPTER I

THE VALUE OF A SOUL

Text: *"For what is a man profited, if he shall gain the whole world, and lose his own soul?"*— Matt. 16:26.

Our Lord Jesus, in this text, introduces us into a realm of values where it is difficult, in fact impossible, for our mathematics to convey accurate conceptions.

If he had compared the value of a human soul to a splendid palace, we might go to the architects and builders who draw plans and erect structures, and get a very correct idea of the amount of money a palace would cost, setting down the figures, and adding up the columns, to ten, fifteen, or twenty millions of dollars; we could say, according to the statement of Jesus Christ, a human soul is worth more than all this.

If Jesus Christ had said, what shall a man be profited if he built, owned and controlled a great city, and lost his own soul, we might figure out, by consulting the proper authorities, something approximating the cost of a great city, with all its manufacturing interests, business center, residential district, its street car system, light plant, waterworks, skyscrapers, and the vast aggregation of material wealth that goes into the making of a great city, climbing into the tens and hundreds of millions, and billions of wealth; then we could add up the figures and say, according to Jesus Christ, a man would make a bad bargain if he possessed himself of a great city and lost his own soul. If Jesus had said, what shall it profit a man, if he gain an entire continent and lose his soul, we would then have a difficult task on our hands if we undertook to figure out, with any sort of accuracy, the value of a continent, with its great farming regions, its mineral resources, its vast forests, its railroad systems and steamship lines, its many investments and industries, its villages, towns and cities. To fix any sort of correct estimate upon such incalculable wealth would be almost impossible.

Come to think of it, a humble farmer cannot tell the actual value of his land. Not long since I was riding with an expert who was employed to locate coal lands. He said to me, up in Virginia there was an old farmer who owned some two hundred acres of land so poor that he could scarcely earn a meager sustenance from its lean and rocky soil. He said on investigation he had found that some hundreds of feet beneath the soil there was a vein of excellent coal, four feet thick, that was worth a vast sum of money, and that a few hundred feet below this vein of coal there was a vein of cannel coal, eleven feet thick, which was so rich that it could be lighted with a match. The farmer little dreamed that his possessions were worth hundreds of thousands of dollars;

that some day the company the expert represented proposed to buy the poor tract of land and gather from beneath its surface the vast treasures of which its owner knew nothing. I remarked to the enthusiastic young expert, that beneath the cannel coal there might be great reservoirs of oil, and beneath the oil marvelous values in gas, and beneath the gas there might be deposits of silver, and beneath the silver, veins of gold, and down deep toward the eternal fires there might be priceless diamonds. He seemed to become amazed and embarrassed as I mentioned the possibilities of wealth beneath the surface of the poor old farm over which he chuckled at the thought of buying. No, it is impossible for us to figure out the value of a continent. It would run into the millions, billions, and hundreds of billions, and yet, we have not reached the value of a soul.

The Lord Jesus Christ was the only being who ever came out of the infinitudes and walked the paths of human life, who really knew the value of a soul. He is the only one who ever walked among us, and talked to us, who has seen a soul, who understands its marvelous capacities, its wondrous beauty and powers. When He came to our earth He saw at once that men had no proper appreciation of soul values. He saw that we thought souls were a very good thing to crowd into the dust and grime of factories and sweatshops, to wear out with incessant toil, to huddle into the deep mines of the earth, and smother with poisonous gases; to march into saloons and degrade with strong drink, that swaggering distillers and brewers may become millionaires; to catch in the traps of white slavery and send away into wretchedness, ruin, and perdition. He saw that man, in his miscalculation, thought that souls were a fine thing to gather from their homes, shops, villages, colleges and universities, throw them into squads, drill them into companies, form them into regiments, weld them into great armies, ship them away from native lands and drive them against rapid-fire guns, hurl them against walls of bayonets, and pour them like a human Niagara into the black pits of outer darkness.

Jesus desired to arrest our attention and awaken in us some sort of proper appreciation of the value of a human soul. He looked about him for a comparison to convey to our minds some conception of its worth. Palaces were as nothing; cities and continents were not large enough; the world itself was too small to convey a correct idea of the fearful blunder a man would make if he should gain this entire planet with the vast wealth on and in it, and lose his own soul.

Think of it! According to the statements of the only One who has ever been in our midst, who has a proper appreciation of values, if you had a scale large enough to put into one end a human soul, and in the other end your prosperous, beautiful little city, and then you put in Louisville, Cincinnati, Cleveland, St. Louis, Kansas

City, Denver, San Francisco, Los Angeles, Houston, New Orleans, Nashville, Charleston, S. C., Richmond, Va., Washington City, Baltimore, Philadelphia, New York, Boston, Glasgow, Scotland, London, Paris, Berlin, St. Petersburg, Bombay, Calcutta, Yokohama, Peking, China, and old Jerusalem—one soul would outweigh them all. Not the soul of Moses, St. Paul, Martin Luther, John Wesley, Wm. Shakespeare, Queen Victoria, Frances Willard, or any other great intellect that ever blessed the world, but the soul of a sick and starving baby in the bony arms of a heathen mother, in the jungles of India.

These words of Jesus awaken in us a thoughtful inquiry into the most interesting subject that can claim our attention. What is a soul? We should not be surprised if, after all, man is God's greatest creation. At the present time no doubt the angels have advantages over us, but they are older than we. As the centuries roll along we may overtake and pass them in the scale of being. We notice that we were created after their creation; and we have not noticed that in His work the Lord tapers down from the larger to the smaller things. After He had created the heavens, and rolled the planets from His finger-tips, and prepared the earth for habitation, He said, "Let us make man in our own image." We have not read in the inspired Book that He spoke thus of any other being He brought into existence. We hear the Psalmist David saying, "When I consider thy heavens, the work of thy fingers, the moon and the stars, which thou hast ordained; What is man, that thou art mindful of him? And the son of man, that thou visitest him? For thou hast made him a little lower than the angels, and hast crowned him with glory and honor. Thou madest him to have dominion over the works of thy hands: thou hast put all things under his feet." We are told that the literal translation of the Hebrew is: "Thou hast made him less than God." We are also taught that angels are our guardians; and Paul tells us that we shall judge angels. Mark you, we are not seeking to depreciate angels, but these words of the Lord Jesus with regard to the value of a soul put one to thinking and wondering where man's place is among the intelligences of of God's creation.

It will be well to remember that the human soul is immortal. We value things on the basis of their durability. After the furnaces of the suns have burned into cinders, and the stars have fallen like the withering leaves of a fig tree, your soul will be rising upon the wings of immortal youth into the glorious heights of a topless heaven and an endless eternity.

The Lord has permitted us to catch some glimpses of the marvelous capacity of the human soul. Some years ago there lived in our community a young negro, an uneducated boy, whose mathematical bump seemed not to have been damaged by the fall. He was a lightning calculator. You could propound to him the most difficult mathematical problems, and almost instantly he would answer you with marvelous accuracy. He did not understand how he did it, but he did it without difficulty. It is possible that, but for sin, we never would have had to learn the multiplication table, or waste time with lead pencil and chalk, knitting our brows over difficult mathematical problems. We are not willing to believe that he was any sort of monstrosity, but by some mysterious means he had the remnant of intellectual power that might have belonged to us all, but for sin.

Many years ago Jenny Lind came to this country. At her first entertainment in Grand Opera in New York, the people paid large sums of money for the privilege of hearing her. She sang until you would forget that you were sick. She sang until you would forget your debts. She sang until you would forget your enemies. She sang until you forgave everybody and loved everybody. She sang until it seemed as if you were lifted into heaven. She sang until she was transfigured before you and seemed to be an angel. We believe if it had not been for sin, had our vocal cords not been jarred out of tune by wicked speech, harsh words and profanity, we would have such singers everywhere. These marvelous gifts and greater await us on yonder golden shore, when we are released from our captivity and come into our own.

Traveling the rugged paths of life, and fighting out the problems on the battlefield here, I have often longed to sing, but have never been able to bring my jargon voice into harmony with sweet melody; but I know that I shall sing. I feel the heavenly anthems within my breast that in yonder world shall break forth in immortal songs of praise. The Scriptures plainly teach that when we have passed through the tragedy of death and the glorious mysteries of the resurrection, we shall rise on the other side in the likeness of our Lord. You remember that Moses went up into the mountain and stayed with God for forty days and nights, and when he came down his countenance shone with such brightness that he must needs be covered with a veil that the people might endure such glory. Suppose he had remained with his God for a year! What must his appearance have been when he descended among the people! Looking into the future state with the prophet's ken, David picked up his harp and sang, "I shall be satisfied when I awake in thy likeness." And John, the Beloved, has written in his Epistle, "Beloved, now are we the sons of God, and it doth not yet appear what we shall be: but we know that when he shall appear, we shall be like him; for we shall see him as he is."

With these Scriptures before us we can begin to appreciate that the spiritual is of infinitely more value than the material; that the immortal is incomparably greater than the transient; that mere dirt, cinders, gold, and diamonds of earth will not compare with that intelligence which lays hold upon the infinite and walks in fellowship and sweet communion with the God of the universe.

The human soul is capable of holiness. It is unthinkable that an infinitely wise and good God would create an immortal, responsible being incapable of a state of moral purity. It must be remembered that sin is not an essential part of human nature. God created man in a state of holiness; sin was introduced into his nature later on. Sin was the work of the devil. Jesus Christ was manifested to destroy the works of the devil. All sin can be eliminated from the soul without the destruction or hurt of any of its essential qualities. The removal of sin leaves the human soul in its normal and original state of purity and oneness with God.

This is the whole purpose and end of the redemptive scheme—to separate from man that which separated him from communion and oneness with his Maker. This is redemption. All prophecy, all priests and sacrifices, all the manifestations and sufferings of the Lord Jesus, all the writings of the Apostles, the great purpose and end of the church is to bring a race, fallen and sinful, back into perfect harmony with the infinite will, and into perfect love of the infinite Being.

If an old man from the backwoods, who never

saw the ocean, who never looked upon a ship, a boat, a skiff, a canoe, or any sort of watercraft, should come out of the woods upon the ocean beach and look with amazement upon the vast expanse of waves; if he should see lying in the sand half buried, a wrecked ship, and if he should ask some old sailor standing by, "What is this object before me?" and the sailor should say, "that is a ship;" the old man from the backwoods would exclaim, "that a ship! Is that what you traverse the sea in? Can you carry commerce and passengers across the vast ocean on that sort of thing?" The old sailor would answer him, "that is a wrecked ship. That is the ruin of a great vessel that went down in triumph, to the sea." The old sailor would tell him of the splendid structure, of its length, and breadth, and depth; of its staunch timbers and iron sides, its graceful masts and powerful engines, and how it plowed the main as a thing of life. Then he would tell him how the storm tossed it, and the waves beat upon it, and the rocks rent it, and the lightning splintered it, and the billows flung it, wrecked, upon the shore. Looking upon that wreck the old man from the woods would have a poor conception of the splendid strength and beauty the great ocean steamer presented before the tempest rent and wrecked it.

Just so it is with man. We have never seen a man. We have seen what is left of him. We have seen him after the waves of sin have dashed

TO CALVARY

him, bruised and broken him along the rocky shores of time. We have seen him after the dirt and sand and grit of sin have been ground into him, defaced and marred him. The Lord Jesus Christ saw him when he came complete in purity and beauty from the creative hand of God. He saw him before he gave a listening ear to the seductive voice of the tempter, before sin had stamped its foul insignia upon his spotless spirit. In that far-off day he was a godlike being. The Son of God loved him with a great, deep, eternal affection, and when he went astray in the paths of sin and ruin, He followed him. Followed him when it meant poverty, suffering, humiliation, a crown of thorns, derision and hatred, the cross with its agony and shame. He followed him like the good shepherd, seeking a lost and wolf-torn sheep, to bind up his wounds and lay him upon the omnipotent shoulders of His mightiness to save to the uttermost.

No price, from the standpoint of the Lord Jesus, was too large to pay; no suffering was too severe to bear; no death agony was too bitter to meet and undergo. Thank God, He solved the problem. He knew the value of human souls and He drank the cup of sorrow and suffering to its last bitter dregs. Standing in the midst of sinful men, He looked back to their original state of purity and godlikeness. He gazed into the eternities of unfolding grace and glory, and as He contemplated man's origin and the possibilities of his redemption and the eternal future—as He weighed these possibilities and destinies He exclaimed, "What shall it profit a man if he shall gain the whole world, and lose his own soul?" At the close of Jesus' mission and ministry, hanging pale and bleeding on a Roman cross, He bowed His head and said, "It is finished." A bridge of redemption and human hope stretched like a mighty arch across the centuries from the fall of Adam in the Garden of Eden to the death of Jesus Christ on the hill of Calvary; over that bridge multitudes and millions have been coming back to God and home to heaven. And when the end shall have come at last, and the immaculate and ever adorable Redeemer shall stand in the midst of those redeemed by the sacrificial blood which He shed upon Calvary's rugged brow, "He shall see of the travail of his soul, and shall be satisfied."

In yonder world when we behold the unfolding, development and progress of human souls—the "exceeding and eternal weight of glory"—we shall be prepared to appreciate more fully the deep meaning of the text, "For what is a man profited if he shall gain the whole world, and lose his own soul?"

CHAPTER II

THE UNIVERSAL CURSE

Text: *"As by one man sin entered into the world, and death by sin; and so death passed upon all men, for that all have sinned."*—Romans 5:12.

The human race is a fallen race. The human heart is defiled by sin. Sin is as universal as human existence. Wherever men are sin is. The prophet Jeremiah covers the ground when he says, "The heart is deceitful above all things, and desperately wicked. Who can know it?" Jer. 17:9. The prophet is not speaking of some individual heart, or the corruption of the nature of some nation or tribe of people; he is speaking of the universal heart, and includes the entire race. All men are fallen and by nature sinful. Their natural tendency is to drift away from God; no man is within himself, naturally holy; holiness must be obtained from some outside source. God must give help and salvation or man must remain a sinner.

Our Lord Jesus Christ speaks very plainly and positively with reference to the sinfulness of human nature and the defilement of the universal heart, when He says, "For from within, out of the hearts of men, proceed evil thoughts, adulteries, fornications, murders, thefts, covetousness, wickedness, deceit, lasciviousness, an evil eye, blasphemy, pride, foolishness; all these evil things come from within and defile the man." Mark 7:21-23. We can have no higher authority than our Lord Jesus, who gives here a fearful description of the human heart, and the history of the world bears witness to the truthfulness of the description our Lord gives. Individual experience is in harmony with what the Lord has to say on this subject. The seed of all sin is in all men and can only be restrained, suppressed, or removed by the grace and power of the Lord Jesus through the operation of the Holy Ghost.

The writings of the Apostle Paul are in perfect harmony with these sayings of the Lord Jesus. In Galatians 5:19-21, Paul describes to us the natural state of the human heart in the following words: "Now the works of the flesh" (that is, the carnal nature, the natural heart), "are manifest, which are these: adultery, fornication, uncleanness, lasciviousness, idolatry, witchcraft, hatred, variance, emulations, wrath, strife, seditions, heresies, envyings, murders, drunkenness, revellings, and such like: of the which I tell you before, as I have also told you in time past, that they which do such things shall not inherit the kingdom of God."

Those persons who deny the natural depravity and sinfulness of the human heart take positive issue with the teachings of Christ and Paul on this important subject. Not only so, but they take a position in conflict with the history of the human race and the experience of the individual Christian. All men of intelligence and piety are well aware of the fact that the greatest battles they have had to fight since their regeneration have been within their own breasts. The "prone to wander, Lord, I feel it" has often been their sad lament.

Christ and the inspired teachers do not mean to say that all men are always under the full domination of their depraved natures; that they are always under the mastery of their evil passions and propensities; but they do teach that all these evil seeds and tendencies are within man, and that they may spring up and break out in any one, or many, of these manifestations at any time. We have false teachers among us who are claiming that the human heart is naturally pure; that there is no such thing as natural depravity or inherited sin. They have a doctrine that all that is necessary in order to a holy character and a righteous life is careful training and helpful environment. There is no place in their theory of religion for the regenerating power of the Holy Spirit, nor for the sanctifying power of Jesus' blood. The teachings of Mrs. Eddy and Pastor Russell are not more dangerous, unscriptural and out of harmony with the teachings of the Scriptures and the stubborn facts of life, than the teaching of those men who strike at the very foundation of all Bible doctrine and the whole structure of our Christianity in their doctrine of the natural moral purity of the human race and therefore no need of the new birth or the divine cleansing; in fact, no need of a blood atonement. It was, and is, because of this fallen and sinful state of the human race that the Atonement became a necessity. Had there been no sin there had been no need of a Saviour. A fallen Adam entailed sin upon a fallen race. There has not been found in all the history of the world a nation, a tribe or a family, or an individual, except our Lord Jesus, who were in and of themselves holy. Wherever we find human beings, we find sinfulness, estrangement from God, and a natural strong current from the divine Father's house. We find everywhere the human heart as Christ has described it, and a manifestation of that depraved heart as Paul has described it. John the Beloved, under the inspiration of the Holy Spirit, is declaring the universal sinfulness of men when he says, "If we say we have no sin, we deceive ourselves and the truth is not in us." 1 John 1:8. John is not here describing the state of those who are saved and sanctified, who by the blood of Christ have been cleansed from all sin, but he is speaking of the universal sinfulness of men and their need of an atonement. Further on, he says, "If we say we have not sinned, we make God a liar and his word is not in us." 1 John 1:10. The whole tenor of the Scriptures unites in teaching this startling truth—that the human race is fallen, the human heart is naturally depraved and sinful. This fact is established by the unerring testimony of three witnesses—the Bible, the history of the race, and the facts in individual experience. It is because of the fall and sinfulness of mankind that Christ was given. The sinfulness of man made the Atonement a necessity. A Redeemer must be found or man is lost without hope; hence, the coming of our Lord Jesus into the world. The fall of man and his sinfulness did not shut him out from the compassionate love of the God who created him, hence, the Atonement. "God so loved the world that he gave his only begotten Son that whosoever believeth in him should not perish, but have everlasting life." John 3:16. The above facts explain at once the reasonableness of the key-note of the gospel of our Lord. "Except a man be born again, he cannot see the kingdom of God." John 3:3. It was to meet the fallen and sinful state of the race that our Lord "suffered without the gate that he might sanctify the people with his own blood." Sin had separated man from God, therefore, sin must be separated from man in order to restore him fully to God. The mission of Jesus Christ in the world is to buy back, redeem, and restore man to a state of obedience, fellowship, harmony and co-operation with God. Sin is not an essential part of man. God did not create man in a state of sin; man became sinful by disobedience; and his sins can be forgiven. The sinful taint and propensity, the carnal nature can be removed and man can be wholly sanctified. The divine image re-stamped upon him, and the man, the whole man, as God created him, can be left in his entirety. Nothing that God created in the make-up of man is taken out of him; or away from him, through the regenerating power and sanctifying grace of our Lord Jesus. Sin was introduced by the devil and our Lord Jesus Christ "was manifested to destroy the works of the devil," and He is abundantly able to save to the uttermost.

In the new birth, or regeneration, pardon is granted; the soul is restored to a justified state, and the guilt of its transgression is cleansed away. A new life principle is imparted, but the sinful propensities are not entirely destroyed; there is yet need of a further cleansing. The Apostle Paul, writing to the Corinthians, says. "And I, brethren, could not speak unto you as unto spiritual, but as unto carnal, even as unto babes in Christ. I have fed you with milk and not with meat; for hitherto ye were not able to bear it, neither yet now are ye able. For ye are yet carnal: for whereas there is among you envying, and strife, and division, are ye not carnal and walk as men?" 1 Cor. 3:1-3. These Corinthians had been pardoned and regenerated. Paul recognizes them as "brethren." He distinctly says they are "babes in Christ." Paul never could, and never would, have recognized one as a "babe in Christ" who had not been born of the Spirit;

such recognition would be impossible. The inspired apostle could make no such mistaken and loose statement. His teaching here is in harmony with the Scriptures and of Christian experience. Christian people everywhere who know they have received the forgiveness of sin, can testify with the Apostle Paul, "I find then a law, that, when I would do good, evil is present with me. But I delight in the law of God after the inward man; but I see another law in my members, warring against the law of my mind and bringing me into captivity to the law of sin within my members." Rom. 8:21-23. We know that the old man, the carnal nature, does not delight in the law of God because the carnal mind (the old man) "is enmity against God; for it is not subject to the law of God neither indeed can be." "So then they that are in the flesh," that is, under the dominion of the old man, "cannot please God." Those who delight in the law of God after the inward man are those who "have put on the new man which is renewed in knowledge after the image of him that created him." This inward man who delights in the law of the Lord is the new man introduced by the new birth who finds himself beset with the inward law of sin which is in his members warring against this new inward man who delights in the law of the Lord. It is this inward law of sin warring against the new man of salvation created by regenerating power that constitutes the *old man* who must be crucified and cast out. The crucifixion of this old man is that entire sanctification that purges and cleanses the heart and restores the soul to its moral state of purity. It is the need of this divine cleansing that the inspired writer has in mind when he says, "Jesus suffered without the gate that he might sanctify the people with his own blood." His sufferings covered the whole sin problem, provided for the forgiveness of our transgressions, regeneration, the introduction of the new man which is created in Christ Jesus, and the crucifixion of the old man, the sinful, carnal nature, and the restoring of the soul to that holiness without which no man shall see the Lord. *Repentance* for sins committed and *faith* in Christ bring forgiveness and the regenerating power of the Holy Spirit. *Consecration* and *trust* in the blood of the everlasting covenant wherewith we are sanctified bring cleansing —purity of heart. Thus it is that sins forgiven, the old man, the carnal nature crucified and cast out, the new man lives in the peace and joy of full salvation under the reign of Christ with the indwelling, comforting and empowering of the Holy Ghost.

This is a great redemption, but Jesus is a great Saviour. Man is a great sinner; his needs are great, but God has provided in Christ all that man needs and requires. Regeneration, or the impartation of the new life, is an act of the Holy Ghost. Sanctification, or the crucifixion of the old man, is an act of the Holy Ghost. Outside of the atonement made by our Lord Jesus on the cross, there is no hope, there is no help. But in Jesus and the Atonement which He has made, there is full redemption, restoration to communion, fellowship and co-operation with God and the blessed indwelling witness of the Holy Ghost. Repentance and faith are man's part; God forgives. Consecration and faith are the acts of the man; God sanctifies wholly. Sin is a fearful fact and is universal. Wherever man is found, sin exists, and the need of salvation exists, but Jesus Christ by the grace of God "hath tasted death for every man;" and Jesus who came to destroy the works of the devil is abundantly able to save us from all sin and present us to his Father "without spot or wrinkle." Keep in mind always the glorious fact that the blood of Jesus Christ, God's Son, cleanseth us from all sin.

CHAPTER III

FULNESS OF REDEMPTION

"*Be ye holy; for I am holy.*"—1 Peter 1:16.
Confucius says, "Heaven means principle." Emerson once remarked, "God Himself cannot procure good for the wicked." In the nature of things there can be no heaven for an unholy soul. To be out of harmony with God, to love what God hates, and to hate what God loves, makes peace with God impossible. This is not a question of theology, philosophy, sectarian prejudice or theories of salvation. In the nature of things, it must be true; it is in harmony with the inevitable logic of the universe.

It is impossible that a soul should be defiled with sin and love of sin and, at the same time, be in harmony with God; and it is unthinkable that a soul could be in peace and joy in this world or any other world and at the same time be out of harmony with God.

The atonement made by Christ is not a provision for men to sin, nor an arrangement by which God may put sinners into heaven. The atonement provides salvation, grace and power to save men from sin, the defilement of it, and the love of it, and to put heaven into them. Christ did not die in order to provide a divine mercy that would enable polluted souls to pass through the gates of Paradise. A merciful God gave His Son to die in order that atonement might be provided to lift sinners into righteousness, to bring them to a state of moral purity so that they are fitted for, because they are in harmony *with*, heaven. One of the highest obligations resting upon the American pulpit is that the living ministry of the present generation dispel from the minds of the people the idea of a sinful Christianity, and that there is a divine mercy that will permit impure, unholy souls to enter with peace into Paradise. Thousands of well-meaning church-members in this nation have been taught that they can live sinful, die happy and enter a holy heaven. They have been taught that holiness of heart and life is impossible. This is a most fearful, dangerous and hurtful heresy. Many people have been taught and believe that Jesus died to make it possible to admit sinners into eternal blessedness; and the effect of such teaching has been most disastrous. The people should be taught everywhere that Jesus did not die so much to save them from hell or to save them in heaven; but He died to save them from sin; salvation from sin makes hell an impossibility and heaven a certainty.

If the ministry of this nation in all evangelical churches should at once assure the people that heaven is impossible to a soul that has not been saved from sin, and that Jesus is abundantly able to save from sin, there would be a powerful revival of religion; at once multitudes would change their entire conception of the plan of redemption and change their conduct, bring their lives into harmony with the teachings of God's Word and cry mightily to Christ for the saving power of His atoning blood.

"Without holiness no man shall see the Lord." This is not only the declaration of Holy Writ, but it is the voice of logic. It is in harmony with the constitution and nature of the human soul. It is unthinkable that an unholy soul could live in a state of bliss in the presence of an infinitely holy God. The whole philosophy of the plan of salvation, the meaning, aim and end of the atonement made by Christ, is that forgiveness may be granted and that the cleansing power of Jesus' blood may bring human souls into a state of forgiveness, purifying and cleansing from all indwelling sin, and bring them into oneness and communion with the blessed Trinity.

It is unthinkable that a holy God could create a sinner or that he could have fellowship with a sinner. Man was created pure. In the use of his free agency he chose to sin. Sin brought separation from God. God could love a sinner, but He could not fellowship with him. He could pity the sinner, He could provide for his redemption, call him to repentance, offer him pardon, provide for him a full and complete atonement, cleanse him from all impurity and bring him back into harmony with Himself.

This was, and is, the great object of the atonement. It was for this purpose that the Lord Jesus came into the world. He was to save men from all sin, to cleanse them from pollution, to take the desire for sin and the love of it out of their natures and to set up within them the Kingdom of God which is "righteousness, and peace, and joy, in the Holy Ghost." The Lord Jesus in the atonement wrought upon the Cross has provided all that God requires and all that man needs. Those who receive the full benefit of the atonement made by Christ need have no fear of death or of coming judgment. It is impossible that Satan could put a stain upon the human soul that Jesus cannot cleanse away. "He is able to do exceeding abundantly, above all that we ask or think." "In him all fulness dwells." Unto Him is given all power in heaven and in earth. He has declared Himself able to give rest to all the burdened race. It is the high note of His Gospel. "Come unto me, all ye that labor and are heavy laden, and I will give you rest." He follows this with, "Whosoever cometh unto me, I will in no wise cast out."

Isaiah, under the inspiration of the Holy Spirit, anticipated the coming and atonement made by Christ and its ample sufficiency to meet all the needs of man, and wrote in his prophecy: "Though your sins be as scarlet, they shall be as white as snow; though they be red like crimson, they shall be as wool." John, the Beloved, looking upon the Christ whom Isaiah had seen in the distant future, says, "The blood of Jesus Christ, his Son, cleanseth us from all sin." The Apostle

Paul rejoices in the fact of this redemption, saying, "I am not ashamed of the Gospel of Christ: for it is the power of God unto salvation to every one that believeth." He further says, "For the law of the Spirit of life in Christ Jesus hath made me free from the law of sin and death. but where sin abounded grace did much more abound." He goes forward declaring that "Now being made free from sin, and become servants to God, ye have your fruit unto holiness and the end everlasting life."

This mission of Christ in the world was to solve the sin problem, to provide an atonement fully equal to the necessities. Sin had separated man from God. He could not be restored to full fellowship and co-operation with God in the plan of the universe and the program of the ages until sin had been separated from him. God cannot change; the sinful man must change or be forever out of harmony with God.

The annunciation angel instructed Mary to call the child *"Jesus,* for he shall save his people from their sins." John, forerunner of our Lord, pointed Jesus out as the "Lamb of God who taketh away the sin of the world." The sacrificial ceremony of the ancient priests, the proclamation of the inspired prophets, and the writings of the holy apostles, all united in exalting our Lord Jesus, mighty to save to the uttermost. This is the message of the ministry. This is the need of the world. Men must be taught the ruin of sin, the blight and destruction it brings into the soul, and the wonderful provision made at such tremendous cost to take sin away, to change man's entire attitude toward sin, to bring him to love what God loves and hate what God hates.

If, beginning with the present, the ministry of the evangelical churches of these United States should declare with great earnestness and zeal that there is not, and cannot be, any harmony with God on earth, or peace with God in heaven, so long as men love sin and commit it, that salvation does not mean submitting to certain ordinances, making a profession of faith and uniting with the church, but it means the forsaking of sin, the shunning of the appearance of evil, and turning to Jesus Christ with all the heart for redemption, for pardon, for cleansing, for freedom from the love of sin and its power,—I say if these truths were preached, this kind of redemption offered, and Jesus Christ lifted up, millions of people would flock to Him for deliverance, revivals would break out and a new era of peace and blessedness would come to our unsettled and disturbed nation. O, that our ministry would cease to ventilate from the pulpit their notions, philosophies, and opinions, and mightily preach the Gospel and offer to the people the Christ of the Gospel. What hunger of soul could be aroused, and the lost people would throng about the great Saviour and touch the hem of His garments of power for salvation.

We have little comprehension of the love of God which gave the Christ to poverty, to humiliation, to suffering, to the mob, to spittle, to the Cross, with all its shame and agony, that we might be redeemed from sin. It's a heart-breaking sorrow that God should have so loved us, paid for us such a marvelous price, that our Lord Jesus should have suffered such shame and agony, and yet the untold millions go on in ignorance of the redemption provided in the Lord Jesus and the glorious possibilities involved in the full and free redemption brought to us in the suffering of the Cross.

Among those who may read this sermon, there are those whose souls are in distress, whose hearts are hungry. Jesus is mighty to save. Let your surrender be complete. Let your consecration be without reservation. Let your faith be without doubt. Lay hold upon Jesus Christ, make Him your Saviour, sanctifier and keeper. Receive the Holy Ghost to indwell and keep you, and give you power, both to live and walk in righteousness before God, and to serve God and humanity in the beauty of holiness.

The text has in it the nature of a commandment. God created the universe. He built our globe. He created man in His own image and likeness. When man fell into sin, God's love followed him and redeemed him at tremendous cost. By creation and redemption, man belongs to God. His love for man gives Him supreme right to call him away from sin, to purity of heart and righteousness of life. The command to be holy is not the stern, harsh voice of tyranny. It is not the arbitrary dictation of a selfish despot. It is the voice of wisdom and love. It is the breaking forth of infinite pity and tender solicitude. It has in it an invitation and a pledge for the highest good. God always provides for the meeting and keeping of His commandments. He commands us to be holy, and on Calvary's rugged Cross He provides for our cleansing from all sin; the most desirable state for a human soul in this universe is freedom from sin. This freedom takes away the fear of Judgment. It turns the deathbed into a chariot of triumph. It opens wide the gates of Heaven. It is a passport to all the unfolding greatness, development and glory of eternal discovery and progress.

Come, let us listen to the commandment of wisdom, the call of love, the entreaty of compassion, the pledge and promise of full redemption and gather about the foot of the Cross of our adorable Redeemer for a full and free deliverance from all sin and that holiness which alone fits us for Heaven, brings us into harmony with God, and makes all eternity an ever-widening and rising blessing of inexhaustible life and glory.

CHAPTER IV

THE REVELATION OF THE TRINITY

Text: *"And be not drunk with wine, wherein is excess; but be filled with the Spirit."* Eph. 5:18.

It will be well for us to remember that in the unfolding of the great plan of redemption, it was divine wisdom that the fulness of the Trinity should be revealed in the following order:
1. The Father.
2. The Son.
3. The Holy Spirit.

The revelation of the Father was, in a remarkable sense, a preparation for the revelation of the Son. The Father revealed Himself to the prophets and revealed to them His plan and purpose for the revelation of His Son. The prophets, in their teachings, prepared the Hebrew Church for the coming of the Son. When Jesus came He bore witness to the inspiration and trustworthiness of the prophecies concerning Himself. He also set His approval upon the whole of the Old Testament Scriptures, as they then existed, the Scriptures we have and believe today, and He, in a most remarkable way, revealed the Father. We never could have had any correct understanding of God, the Father, had not Jesus come and given us a revelation of Him. It was Jesus who taught us that, "God so loved the world that he gave his only begotten Son that whosoever believeth in him should not perish, but have everlasting life." It was Jesus who forgave the woman who was being dragged to be stoned to death for fearful sin and said to her, "Go, and sin no more." It was Jesus who spoke peace and gave assurance to a dying thief that he should be with Him in Paradise the very day of their death upon the Cross, and added to all this, "He that hath seen me hath seen the Father." What a marvelous revelation Jesus gave of the God of the Universe! We never could have had any accurate conception of God had not Jesus come. In fact, Jesus taught that "No man knoweth the Father save the Son and he to whom the Son will reveal him." He said, "No man cometh to the Father but by me."

It was our Lord Jesus Christ who prepared the Church for the coming of the Holy Spirit. Jesus in the flesh was comparatively local throughout His life ministry upon the earth. His life in the flesh was circumscribed to a very small part of the world's geography. It was in part because of this fact that He said, "It is expedient," that is, "better for you," that I go away.

The ministry of Jesus was full of teaching with reference to the Holy Spirit, His Person, His equal in honor and power with the Father and the Son, and in His concern and work in the salvation of men. The Holy Spirit was to be world-wide in His presence and influence. He was to touch men everywhere at the same time. The coming of the

Holy Spirit was the climax of revelation. It was one of the greatest epochs in the history of God's dealings with men. Man was created for God. Sin brought separation. The coming of the Holy Spirit to indwell men was a marvelous restoration of communion and fellowship between men and the blessed Trinity.

It is an interesting fact that each person of the Trinity reveals the other person of the Trinity, that is, while we had the revelation of the Father before we had the revelation of the Son, and never could have had any correct understanding of the Father if the Son had not come and revealed Him, even so we shall not be able to have anything like a correct comprehension of the Lord Jesus Christ without the coming of the Holy Spirit. The Holy Spirit reveals, explains, exalts and glorifies the Lord Jesus Christ. The Apostle evidently has this in mind when he says, "No man calleth Jesus Lord but by the Holy Spirit." The Holy Spirit exalts Jesus high over all. Those persons who have been baptized by the Holy Ghost are entirely safe from any of the shallow conceptions or false teachings of Unitarianism. They are fixed forever in their abiding faith in the Lord Jesus Christ. Those who have received the Holy Spirit have gotten such a revelation of Jesus that they have no trouble in believing in the Virgin Birth, the Godhead, the sinless life, the absolute truth of the teachings of Jesus and the atoning merit of His suffering, of His triumphant, bodily resurrection, and His existence and intercessions at the right hand of the Father, His power to forgive sins, to cleanse and sanctify souls. The baptism with the Holy Spirit is a tremendous epoch in the history of a child of God and wonderfully confirms and establishes the faith of those who reeive Him in His in-coming, cleansing, and abiding.

How wonderful it is that the third Person of the Trinity, one and equal with the Father, should come to abide, to comfort, illuminate, and empower the child of God for service. We can think of nothing more marvelous in the scheme of redemption than that God, from whom we were separated by sin, should separate us from sin through the merit of our blessed Lord and Saviour and come to indwell us. With what diligence, humility, self-examination, and earnestness we should pray, wait, long for and receive the Holy Spirit, and having received Him how humbly we should walk in obedience to His blessed guidance.

There is this that should be remembered carefully. The Holy Spirit will never guide us into any teaching or action out of harmony with the plain teachings of the Word of God. This should be a final test in all impressions and leadings and if we should be impressed to feel led to say or do anything that contradicts the Word of God, as taught in Old Testament and New Testament Scriptures, we must conclude at once that it is not the leading or impression of the Holy Spirit. He is always and absolutely true to the Scriptures and the teachings of Jesus.

In the Epistle to the Ephesians, from which we have selected our text, we find constant reference to the Holy Spirit, His presence and His holy offices in the Church of God and the individual child of God. It is in this Epistle that we learn that we are "sealed with the Holy Spirit of promise." It is here we are taught that through Christ we have "access by one Spirit unto the Father" and "are built upon the foundation of the apostles and prophets, Jesus Christ himself being the chief cornerstone; in whom all the building fitly framed together groweth unto an holy temple in the Lord, in whom ye also are builded together for an habitation of God through the Spirit." Eph. 2:20, 21, 22. It is in this wonderful Epistle that the Apostle gives us a description of the result of the indwelling of the Holy Spirit, saying, "For the fruit of the Spirit is in all goodness and righteousness and truth, proving what is acceptable unto the Lord."

Immediately following the text, in which we are commanded, "Be not drunk with wine, wherein is excess; but be filled with the Spirit," the Apostle goes on showing the result of such filling. He says, "Speaking to yourselves in psalms and hymns and spiritual songs, singing and making melody in your hearts to the Lord, giving thanks always for all things unto God and the Father in the name of our Lord Jesus Christ."

How blessed is such an experience. What more could we ask than that the great scheme of redemption provides for the forgiveness of all our transgressions, the cleansing away of all our unrighteousness, and the indwelling of the Holy Spirit to bear witness to the truth of God's Word, to the Deity and saving and sanctifying power of the Lord Jesus Christ? Then, let us see to it that we be filled with the Spirit, that we be intoxicated with the indwelling and empowering of the Holy Spirit, who shall bring into us the spirit of the Lord Jesus, who shall make us more and more like the blessed Christ, ever remembering that the spirit of Christ is the spirit of holy courage, that would bear witness to the truth and who knew it meant the cruelty of the Cross, and a spirit of forgiveness and pity that could pardon and pray for those who nailed Him there. The indwelling of the Holy Spirit means that we shall become wonderfully Christlike in our absolute faith in the Eternal Father, His Word, and blessedly submissive to His will, and, at the same time, greatly concerned for the salvation of the people, always bearing about with us an attitude of pity, humility and mercy and love, even for our enemies. O that we may know what it means to be filled *with*, comforted and empowered *by*, the indwelling of the Holy Spirit.

CHAPTER V

AN UTTERMOST SALVATION

Text: *"Wherefore he is able also to save them to the uttermost that come unto God by him, seeing he ever liveth to make intercession for them."* Heb. 7:25.

It is a good long journey from the ugly bulb to the beautiful and fragrant bloom but if the bulb is brought in contact with the proper elements it will decay and pass away; but the bloom, waving its beauty, will scatter its fragrance on the wind. There must be soil, sunshine and shower transforming the bulb into the bloom. If the means are not used the end cannot be secured. The bulb will shrivel, decay, and there will be no bloom.

There is a wide difference between the sinner, in rebellion against God, and the saint in communion with Him; and yet so certain as there are conditions that can change the bulb to blossoms, there are forces that can transform the sinner into the saint. "The gospel is the power of God unto salvation to every one that believeth."

There was a wide difference between the young man, John Bunyan, so vulgar and profane, that sinners sought to restrain him from his extreme wickedness, and John Bunyan, the mighty man of God, who trod the gloomy aisles of Bedford jail for twelve long years, imprisoned for Jesus' sake who, when they offered to release him on condition that he would not preach, gave answer, "I will stay in this dungeon until the moss grows upon my forehead like my eyebrows; but you may turn me out of this prison today and I will preach Jesus Christ tomorrow." In his case the bulb of the blasphemous sinner had passed, and the saint was in full flower.

What was the secret of it all? What the transforming power? One day John Bunyan, in the depths of his sins, looked up and a wonderful vision was before his eyes; it was as if he beheld the Christ hanging in His blood and agony upon the cross. Bunyan gazed in wonder and alarm; the power of sin was broken; the mask was torn from him, and sin appeared in all of its distortion and hideousness. He fought a long, hard battle with doubts and fears and Satan. He wallowed in the mire of "the slough of despond," but he finally struggled out and came to the cross. His burden fell off and the Sun of righteousness arose upon him, and the flower of faith and love burst forth into fulness of unfading beauty and fragrance.

What a transforming from the Jerry McAuley of the criminal row in Sing Sing Prison to the Jerry McAuley preaching Christ, and winning souls to Christ, bringing up men from the depths of the slums into the white light of the great salvation in a mission in New York City. Who wrought the change? It was Jesus, the same Jesus who made the blind to see, the deaf to hear, who caused the lame to leap for joy, and the dead to rise up and come forth from the tomb. He touched the dirty, decaying bulb of sin and it burst forth into the beautiful flower of salvation. St. Paul, who writes himself down as the "chief of sinners," was a most unlikely convert to Christianity, a learned, proud, prejudiced Jew, full of self-conceit, so blinded in his soul that he believed himself to be doing the will of God when he haled to prison and even gave consent to the death of the saints, is suddenly changed from the persecutor of the disciples of Christ to the powerful preacher of the gospel of Christ. What wrought this marvelous transformation? Approaching Damascus yonder he saw a light and heard a voice; the light was the glory of Christ, and the voice was that of our Redeemer, and the persecutor becomes the champion of the cross and rejoices in the privilege to suffer for his Lord. The marvelous transformations wrought among sinful men by our Lord Jesus written down, would fill great libraries full of books.

It was the mission of Jesus in the world to seek and to save the lost. All power is given unto Him; all devils flee at His rebuke. The thunder of the tempest is hushed at His command; the trembling harlot goes from His presence forgiven, in purity and peace. His mighty arm lifts the dying thief from the cross into paradise. In His hands a boy's luncheon is multiplied into a feast for hungry thousands. Why not? Those hands had laid the foundations of the universe. They had scooped out the beds of the ocean and piled the mountains to the clouds. They had unrolled the plains and stretched out the vast blue sky. The moon and stars were the work of His fingers, the vast regiments of blazing suns had come into existence at His call and marched in splendid order at His command. He sits upon the throne of His glory; angels worship at His feet, but He is not content. He saw man in his original purity; He knew him before he had listened to the sedective voice of the tempter, ere sin had stamped its foul insignia upon his spotless spirit. He had loved him with a love that could not let him go. He came to redeem him from his sins, to lift him from his fall, to restore him to holiness, fellowship and communion with God. All the power of the eternal Godhead that had created angels, built the universe, set millions of circling suns in their unending course, had come down to rescue man from his captivity to sin. He came armed with all power over devils, disease and death; the very elements are obedient to His word; death is His submissive slave. He is able to save to the uttermost.

We must not think of Jesus simply as having come into the world and died for the redemption of souls, and returned to the Father, but we must remember that He is the same Christ, that He "ever liveth to make intercession unto God" for the souls for whom He suffered, the sinners He redeemed in the agonies of the cross. We are in danger of looking back through the centuries and thinking of the Babe of Bethlehem, the young Carpenter of Nazareth, the wonderful Teacher on the seaside, the marvelous Preacher in the prow of the boat, with the multitude before Him on the seashore, the crucified victim of the cross, and of forgetting that Jesus is alive forevermore, that He loves the souls of men with the same passion that characterized Him when He prayed for those who crucified Him, when He answered the prayer of the dying thief upon the cross. He announces His victory over death. He says, "I am alive forevermore." He declares that all power in heaven and earth is given unto Him.

The inspired apostle assures us in the text that "He is able to save them to the uttermost that come unto God by him." It must not be forgotten that the sinner's part is to "come." He must find the return road of repentance. The wicked must forsake his way; the sinner must give up his sinful thoughts, he must break with his godless companions, he must be glad to renounce his sins and he must realize that the only way back to God is through Jesus Christ. There is no way of salvation apart from Jesus. God has shut up redemption in His Son, and this redemption is ample. It meets all the needs of a death for every man: "Whosoever will may come," and we have the assurance that he who comes will in no wise be cast out.

Jesus did not only pray in the Garden of Gethsemane with the burden of lost humanity upon Him, and on the cross of His agony, "Father, forgive them, they know not what they do," but He continues to pray for us. Oh, wonderful thought! "He ever liveth to make intercession for them that come unto God by him." On the mediatorial throne somewhere in the vast depth of the universe there is a city, a place of habitation, a house of many mansions, a throne of infinite power, a God of love, and there in His presence is an interceding Saviour. He pleads for those He represents. He has borne the sins of a lost world in His body on the cross, and now on the mediatorial throne He remembers us; He reminds infinite wisdom, awful justice, and the great source of all blessing and grace, that He has paid our debt, that He has suffered in our stead, that He has made an atonement for our sins, and He never fails to secure forgiveness, justification, adoption, peace and eternal life for all those who come unto God by Him.

Let us comfort our hearts that we have a living Christ before our Father; that He hears our prayers, that He joins His intercession with ours, that the Father hears Him, and never will forget His covenant with His Son; that if He would take our sins and die in our stead, we should have forgiveness if we would repent, and return to God, trusting in the atonement made for us by His Son, our blessed Lord and Saviour.

What more could mercy do? Where is there any room for improvement in this great scheme which offers a full and free salvation to all men? Let us tell the good news to the whole world that Jesus Christ has come and solved the sin problem, that He has made an atonement for the sins of the whole world, that He ever liveth to make intercession, that He can secure a hearing for us, and a full and free pardon. Oh, that men would come to God by Him, believing on Him, trusting in Him, accepting the atonement He has made, and enter by Him into the presence of a reconciled God, come back into peace, and purity, and companionship with the blessed Trinity.

CHAPTER VI

BABES IN CHRIST

Text: *"And I, brethren, could not speak unto you as unto spiritual, but as unto carnal, even as unto babes in Christ. I have fed you with milk, and not with meat; for hitherto ye were not able to bear it, neither yet now are ye able."* 1 Cor. 3:1, 2.

The doctrine of entire sanctification as a gracious work of grace wrought in the hearts of God's children, subsequent to regeneration, rests upon a firm scriptural foundation. Not only is this true, but these scriptures are corroborated by the actual experience of devout Christian people.

If the Scriptures taught that regeneration destroyed all sinful inclination, tendencies and bent to evil, the Christian would find within himself a contradiction of such teaching and would be distressed to find the experiences of his heart in conflict with the teaching and tone of apostolic writing. Fortunately, there is no such conflict.

In our text, as repeatedly in the writings of the Apostle Paul, and others of the New Testament writers, we find instruction, warnings and exhortations with reference to indwelling sin. As we search the Scriptures we find that in the atonement wrought by our Lord Jesus upon the cross, there has been provided a gracious deliverance from this carnal nature.

In the work of redemption and preparation for a life of service, and a home in heaven, there are two very distinct works of grace for each individual. First, regeneration, and second, sanctification. These are very different operations of the Holy Spirit. Regeneration is the *impartation of a new life;* sanctification is the *expurgation of an old life.* Along with regeneration come pardon, justification and the cleansing away of guilt of sins committed, and adoption into the family of God. In His teaching, our Lord Jesus Christ calls this blessed work of regenerating grace, being "born again." It is by this operation of the Holy Spirit that one is made, in Christ, a new creature.

Sanctification is different, in that it involves a death. Note the words used: Born—crucified. The first is the coming of a new life; the second is the crucifixion of an old life. We read from the Apostle Paul in Rom. 6:6, "Knowing this, that our old man is crucified with him (Christ) that the body of sin might be destroyed, that henceforth we should not serve sin."

It is this old man, this body of sin, that is cleansed away by a gracious fiery baptism with the Holy Ghost in sanctification. The reader will note that in the use of the word sanctification we are not thinking of sanctification in any legal sense, as a mere setting apart of some object or person for divine service, but we are thinking of it as defined by Webster, when he tells us "a

TO CALVARY 51

sanctifying, or being sanctified, or made holy; an act of God's grace by which men's affections are purified and exalted   To free from sin, to purify."

The reader will note that in his definition Mr. Webster is here defining sanctification in its highest evangelical sense. It is unfortunate that in studying the Scriptures any one should conclude that the word sanctification is always to mean simply to set apart, and never to mean to cleanse and make holy. It is in this higher sense that we are thinking as we use the word sanctification in this sermon.

In Hebrews 13:12, we read: "Wherefore Jesus also, that he might sanctify the people with his own blood, suffered without the gate." This is in beautiful harmony with John's Epistle, First chapter, 7th verse. "But, if we walk in the light, as he is in the light, we have fellowship one with another, and the blood of Jesus Christ his Son cleanseth us from all sin."

It is quite safe to say that the great objective of the atonement that God has made for sin in the offering of His Son upon the cross, was our complete deliverance from all sin inherited, and all sins committed. In the divine order the forgiveness of the sins we have committed comes before the cleansing of the carnal nature—the inherited body of sin.

Paul states it this way: "Knowing this, that our old man is crucified with him, that the body of sin might be destroyed, that henceforth we should not serve sin." Rom. 6:6. Describing what follows, in the same chapter, 22nd verse, we read, "But now being made free from sin, and become servants to God, ye have your fruit unto holiness, and the end everlasting life."

Commenting on the same scripture which furnishes our text, Mr. Wesley, the founder of the Methodist Church, said: "Sanctification begins in the moment a man is justified. Yet sin remains in him, yea, the seed of all sin, till he is sanctified throughout." Again Mr. Wesley says, "There does still remain, even in them that are justified, a mind, which is in some measure carnal; so the apostle tells even the followers at Corinth, 'Ye are carnal;' a heart bent to backsliding, still ever ready to depart from the living God; a propensity to pride, self-will, anger, revenge, love of the world, yea, and all evil; a root of bitterness, which, if the restraint were taken off for a moment, would instantly spring up; yea, such a depth of corruption as, without clear light from God, we cannot possibly conceive."

Reading farther, we find Mr. Wesley saying, "We may learn the mischievousness of that opinion, that we are wholly sanctified when we are justified; that our hearts are then cleansed from all sin. It is true, we are then delivered from the dominion of outward sin, and, at the same time, the power of inward sin is so broken that we need no longer follow or be led by it; but it is by no means true that inward sin is then totally destroyed, that the root of pride, self-will, anger, love of the world, is then taken out of the heart."

In our text the apostle is in perfect harmony with what we have quoted from Mr. Wesley. Perhaps it were better to say, that Mr. Wesley is in perfect harmony with the Apostle Paul, who states very clearly that the Corinthians to whom he writes are "babes in Christ." They were able to take milk. They could not have been babes in Christ if they had not been born again. The case is very clear; they had been born of the Spirit; they were "babes in Christ;" they were taking spiritual nourishment, but they were not ready for the stronger meat to promote their better spiritual growth, for, says the apostle, "Ye are yet carnal."

The Holy Scriptures clearly teach that even Christians, God's children, do have in them this carnal nature, this old man, up to the time of his crucifixion; this strange something which is at enmity against God, greatly retards spiritual growth and hinders Christian activity. This teaching of the Scriptures harmonizes with Christian experience. It is clearly set forth in the hymnology of the church, in systematic theology, in biology, and the autobiography of Christian experience.

Who has ever been a broken-hearted penitent and experienced the pardoning mercy of God, along with the witness of the Spirit to adoption into the family of the Eternal Father, who has not been startled to find strangely rising up in him thoughts, desires, inclinations, and emotions that were utterly hateful, and that sometimes made the believing heart to cry out, "Who shall deliver me from this body of death!"

The apostle tells us that it is through the crucifixion of the old man that this body of sin—the body of death—is destroyed. Thanks be to God, there is deliverance through our crucified and risen Lord, whose blood cleanseth from all sin, who is able to save to the uttermost.

Throughout the history of early Methodism this great doctrine of entire sanctification was central in the ministry of Mr. Wesley, his coadjutors, and the preachers under his direction and guidance. Everywhere they went they urged sinners to repent and believers to hasten on to entire sanctification. They were assured that this gracious work of the Spirit was instantaneous; that it was received by faith in the all-atoning blood of the Lord Jesus. Every Methodist convert was taught, stirred and stimulated to press on at once for this perfect cleansing and the perfect love which came into the heart when the old carnal nature was crucified and cast out. This desire and faith, with so great a promise, were a wonderful protection against backsliding and worldliness of any kind. It created in the minds of the young converts a divine urge, a "hungering and thirsting after righteousness," a pressing on with intense desire until the fulness of the blessing of the gospel of Christ was received and the soul was established in faith and purity. It rested in blessed communion with the Holy Trinity, and was filled with an unquenchable zeal to bring the lost to Christ and help believers into the Canaan of perfect love. If our church literature called upon our people to repeat the history, experience and power of the early Methodists; if our bishops, editors, college presidents, presiding elders, district superintendents, pastors, lay leaders and Sunday school teachers, were aflame with this perfect love that burned and blazed in the sanctified hearts of the founders of Methodism, there would burst out in this nation such a revival as has never been known since the crucifixion of our Lord. People would respond to such preaching, exhortation and leadership by thousands and by millions, and hungry hearts of other denominations would crowd our altars and pray and press into full redemption from sin. The salt of divine truth would permeate our religious, social, political and economic life; the light of holy living and glad testimony would illuminate the world and bring Protestantism into a new era of religious history.

The blessing of such a line of action, with its gracious results, would touch and stir every nation beneath the sun, and untold millions of immortal souls would be gathered into the kingdom of God through the saving power of our Lord Jesus. If such a revival is not experienced, the blame cannot be laid to a lack of love of the Father, or any defect in the redemptive power of the sacrificial sufferings of Christ, or indifference and inactivity of the Holy Spirit. The blame now, throughout the years, and at the judgment bar, must rest on the leaders in the church, and the men in the pulpits who fail to declare the whole counsel of God.

Oh, for an awakening that will arouse and stir the ministry of this nation and bring them to offer to the people the wonderful provision of the gospel which presents us a Christ abundantly able to *save all men from all sin.*

CHAPTER VII

THE CARNAL MIND AND ITS CURE

Text: *"The carnal mind is enmity against God: for it is not subject to the law of God, neither indeed can be. So then they that are in the flesh cannot please God. But ye are not in the flesh, but in the Spirit, if so be that the Spirit of God dwell in you."* Rom. 8:7-9.

What is the carnal mind, which the apostle says is "enmity against God?" It will be helpful to us in answering this question to notice the various names given in the Scriptures to this something in human nature out of harmony with all good, and at war with God. In Rom. 6:6, it is called "our old man." In the same verse, it is referred to as "the body of sin." In Rom. 7:20, it is mentioned as "sin that dwelleth in me." Frequently it is called the "flesh."

It must be understood that the word *flesh* here does not refer to the meat on our bones; the body in which we live. The apostle was addressing living things and he says, "But ye are not in the flesh, but in the Spirit." It will be seen at once that the term *flesh* refers to the carnal nature—the indwelling sin.

Let us bear in mind that all references to the "old man," the "body of sin," "indwelling sin," the "carnal mind," and sinful flesh refer to one and the same thing, and that thing is our inherent sinful nature which makes us prone to wander from God, to violate His law, to go into rebellion against Him.

We must make a distinction here between sin and sinning. Sin is a condition, a natural, unholy state, an indwelling corrupt principle. Sinning is an unholy action. It is wrong doing. There may be sin in a man who is not actually sinning. Evil appetites and passions may be restrained and controlled so they do not break out in actual violation of God's law. It requires careful and earnest prayer to restrain, subdue, and hold the carnal nature in subjection. It is almost certain at times to break out in actual transgression.

The carnal mind is as universal as the human race. All men are by nature sinful. All have suffered because of the fall. Let us notice the nature of the carnal mind. Gal. 5:19-21: "Now the works of the flesh are manifest which are these: Adultery, fornication, uncleanness, lasciviousness, idolatry, witchcraft, hatred, variance, emulations, wrath, strife, seditions, heresies, envyings, murders, drunkenness, revellings, and such like: of the which I tell you before, as I have also told you in time past, that they that do such things shall not inherit the kingdom of God."

This is a fearful picture presented by the Apostle Paul, but it is not overdrawn. It is not only in harmony with the general tenor of Bible teaching, but it is descriptive of the history of the race. It is not only true of the people who live in the jungles, but it is true of those who have lived in palaces and kings' courts. All sorts of beastly sins are not only found in the slums but in the mansion on Fifth Avenue. Murder, theft, adultery, debauchery and outbreaking sins of every kind are found in every class of society; not only among the illiterate, but among the highly educated also.

The teachings of our Lord and Master are in perfect harmony with the Apostle Paul. Let Jesus describe the natural state of the human heart. Mark 7:21-23: "For from within, out of the heart of men, proceed evil thoughts, adulteries, fornications, murders, thefts, covetousness, wickedness, deceit, lasciviousness, an evil eye, blasphemy, pride, foolishness: All these things come from within, and defile the man."

It will be seen at once that there is no difference or conflict in the teachings of the Apostle Paul and of our Lord and Master. Jesus here gives us a true portrait of the human heart. The carnal mind is not destroyed in regeneration. The inspired apostle, in his first Epistle to the Corinthians, third chapter, first, second and third verses, very clearly points out the fact that these newly regenerated believers had in them the carnal nature. "And I, brethren, could not speak unto you as unto spiritual, but as unto carnal, even as unto babes in Christ. I have fed you with milk, and not with meat: for hitherto ye were not able to bear it, neither yet now are ye able. For ye are yet carnal: for whereas there is among you envying, and strife, and divisions, are ye not carnal, and walk as men?"

This teaching is very clear. These Corinthians had experienced the new birth. They were babes in Christ. It were impossible for them to be babes in Christ without the new birth; but they were yet carnal, and their carnality was manifesting itself in disagreements and contention. When St. Paul cries out against the "sin that dwelleth in me" he is speaking of the common state of God's regenerated children. He is very specific. He says: "Now if I do that I would not, it is no more I that do it, but sin that dwelleth in me."

The carnal mind—indwelling sin—is not an essential part of human nature. God did not create it. It was introduced by Satan; it can be eliminated and the whole God-created man remain intact. Regeneration is the impartation of a new nature. Sanctification is the expurgation of an old nature. These are two great works of grace. The figures of speech used to designate these two gracious works are entirely different, wide apart. Jesus takes birth to convey the correct idea of regeneration. "Ye must be born again." It is the incoming of a new life.

The Apostle Paul in speaking of the destruction of the carnal nature uses the figure exactly opposite to that of birth. "Knowing this, that our old man is crucified with him, that the body of sin might be destroyed, that henceforth ye should not serve sin." Rom. 6:6. You will notice at once the very wide difference of the two works of grace, the incoming of the new life, which is a birth, and the outgoing of the old carnal life, which is a death, a crucifixion. When the Apostle Paul tells us to "put off the old man" he has in mind this carnal nature, "which is corrupt according to the deceitful lusts." When he tells us to "put on the new man, which after God is created in righteousness and true holiness," he is thinking of the regenerating power of the Holy Ghost making us in Christ new creatures.

These Scriptures are in perfect harmony with Christian experience. Not a Christian here and there, now and then, but with all Christians throughout the history of the church; God's children who know positively that they have repented, that they have forsaken sin, been graciously regenerated and received the witness of the Spirit know also that they have had bitter struggles against inward uprisings of evil desires, carnal impulses and have had to battle against these impulses, sometimes crying out with the Apostle Paul, "O wretched man that I am! Who shall deliver me from the body of this death!"

Thank God, there is deliverance from the carnal nature. The old man can be crucified. The atonement provided by our Lord Jesus secures for us not only the forgiveness of our actual sins, but it also provides for the cleansing of our hearts from indwelling sin. The body of sin can be destroyed. The Apostle says, "But ye are not in the flesh, if so be that the Spirit of God dwelleth in you." He did not mean that they were not yet in the body, but he meant they were not under the dominion of the carnal nature. The coming in of the Holy Ghost is the outgoing of the old man. If the strong man of God, the Holy Ghost, keeps the house the old man is not only cast out, but he is kept out.

Suffer a word of exhortation: Have you experienced the regenerating power of the Holy Spirit? Have you had inward uprisings and desires contrary to the spiritual life? Have you prayed and fought against unholy thoughts and appetites striving for the mastery? How strange! You know you have been converted; you love God, His truth and His people, yet this inward foe presses you sorely; you are often in great distress; your faith is crippled, your love grows cold. You are grieved at your lack of zeal. You cannot understand yourself. You fully realize the statement contained in the text that your carnal nature is enmity against God.

The blood of Jesus Christ, God's Son, cleanseth us from all sin. It is not the will of God that His people should be hindered and harrassed by this old man, this indwelling, perverse nature. The Lord Jesus can master him, the Holy Ghost can come in, purifying the heart by faith, taking up His abode and abiding, keeping the soul in peace

TO CALVARY 63

and security. A thousand evils may press without but Jesus dwells within. He is the strong man that can keep His house bought with His precious blood, against all the power of the enemy. This is a blessed experience; it is a little heaven in the heart. It brings within a full assurance of faith, it gives one songs in the night. Would the reader have this experience? It is a divine gift. Our part is consecration; to yield ourselves without reservation into the mighty hands of Him who loved us and gave Himself for us, and to trust without doubt in the all-cleansing power of the atoning blood shed for us on Calvary's rugged cross. Let us have boldness to enter into the fulness of the blessing of the gospel of Christ; to dare to trust Him and to plunge by faith into the fountain that cleanseth from all sin.

CHAPTER VIII

TRAITS OF CARNALITY

Text: *"For whereas there is among you envying, and strife, and divisions, are ye not carnal, and walk as men?"*—1 Cor. 3:3.

A careful reading of this third chapter of First Corinthians will reveal the fact that the Apostle Paul is seeking to allay contention, strife, and division among the Christians at Corinth. He has learned that some of these young converts to the faith in Christ are claiming Paul as their spiritual leader and others are rallying about Apollos. He calls their attention to the fact that Apollos and he were only agents in the hands of God, Paul planting, Apollos watering, but God alone giving the increase. He insists that Jesus, and Jesus only, is the foundation of our faith and salvation, and no man can lay any other.

It is our purpose to notice the cause of the dissension and strife among these Corinthian Christians which Paul very clearly points out. He does not hint that they are not converted; he admits that they are babes in Christ, which shows that they have been born again. They were not babes physically; having been born of the Spirit they were in their spiritual babyhood. Being born again they had become children of God, but notwithstanding this fact there were divisions and strife among them and, in our text, the Apostle points out the cause—they were "yet carnal."

Careful and accurate diagnosis is one of the most important items in the treatment of all physical diseases; without knowing the *cause* of the sickness, the physician may administer a medicine that would hinder, instead of help, in the cure of his patient. St. Paul was an inspired diagnostician of spiritual diseases; he fully understood the cause which lay at the root of the distractions and divisions among the young Christians at Corinth. They were "yet carnal." There was in them a root sin from which these outward evils sprang and manifested themselves.

In order that we may better understand the nature of this malady and the treatment necessary, let us seek further information from Paul on the subject of carnality. It will be found that the Apostle has much to say about the carnal nature remaining in the children of God. He has a number of names for this inward evil; sometimes he calls it, "sin that dwelleth in me;" sometimes he names it, "the old man," and at other times he denominates it, "the flesh." In the text, it is "carnal"—the carnal mind. Looking into the subject we find that all of these names refer to the same thing, that they never refer to the acts of the Christian, but always to an inward state, or condition, which may lead to improper action; an inward nature, the whole tendency of which is to manifest itself in sinful deeds.

We observe that this carnal nature is something that must be restrained and kept inactive in order to retain a state of justification; that it is so aggressive and active it is very difficult to control, and that to be delivered from all sin and the strong likelihood of many outbreaks, it must be cleansed out and cast away in order to entire sanctification—the indwelling and abiding of the Holy Ghost.

In Romans 8:6, 7, we find Paul saying, "For to be carnally minded is death; but to be spiritually minded is life and peace. Because the carnal mind is enmity against God; for it is not subject to the law of God, neither indeed can be." From this declaration of the Apostle we learn that the Corinthian Christians had an element of death in their life; that the carnal mind in them about which the Apostle is so solicitous was in rebellion against God and was of a nature that it could not be subject to Him. It is of vast importance that we know something of this strange inward state which was causing division and strife among God's children; this something that is not, and cannot, be subject to God.

If we turn to Galatians 5:17, we find that this carnal, or flesh nature, which is not subject to God, is also at war against the Holy Spirit:—"For the flesh, (carnal nature) lusteth against the Spirit, and the Spirit against the flesh; (carnal nature) and these are contrary the one to the other; so that ye cannot do the things that ye would." A little further on in this same chapter, we find a graphic pen picture of this inward antagonist

TO CALVARY

to spiritual life which the Apostle denominates the *flesh*. He makes no reference to the meat on your bones, but to the carnal, sinful something in the heart. Follow the Apostle in Gal. 5:19-21, as he describes the *flesh life* and the *Spirit life* in contrast with each other.

"Now the works of the flesh (carnal nature) are manifest, which are these; adultery, witchcraft, hatred, variance, emulation, wrath, strife, seditions, heresies, envyings, murders, drunkenness, revellings, and such like: of the which I tell you before, as I have told you in time past, that they which do such things shall not inherit the kingdom of God." It must be understood that this carnal nature is not in *rulership* over a *regenerated soul*, but neither is this carnal nature entirely cleansed out in the act of regeneration. Paul has already shown us that one may be born of the Spirit—be a babe in Christ—and, at the same time be "yet carnal."

The contrast between the full life of the Spirit and this carnal life is most striking, as seen in the picture in this same chapter, verses 22 to 25: "But the fruit of the Spirit is love, joy, peace, longsuffering, gentleness, goodness, faith, meekness, temperance; against such there is no law. And they that are Christ's have crucified the flesh with the affections and lusts. If we live in the Spirit, let us also walk in the Spirit." Note the Apostle says, "They that are Christ's have crucified the flesh," that is, the (carnal nature) "with the affections and lusts." The young Corinthian Christians had been pardoned; they had been regenerated, but they had not yet been wholly sanctified. They had not yet crucified "the flesh with its affections and lusts."

In order that you may see that St. Paul has not overdrawn the picture of the fallen, carnal heart of man, we call attention to the words of our Lord Jesus found in Mark 7:21-23: "For from within, out of the heart of men, proceed evil thoughts, adulteries, fornications, murders, thefts, covetousness, wickedness, deceit, lasciviousness, an evil eye, blasphemy, pride, foolishness: All these evil things come from within, and defile the man." Our Lord Jesus says emphatically that all these evil things come from within and defile the man. They could not come from within if they were not there. They are there, entailed from the fallen and sinful nature of our federal head. "As in Adam all die, so in Christ shall all be made alive." All along the stream of human life there has been much inheritance of corruption from the turbid tides of sin; the whole race has felt its defilement.

We must now turn back to Galatians 5:22-24, calling your attention to one word that has already been mentioned in this last verse quoted above. It is a significant word loaded down with profound meaning. It is the word, *"Crucified."* This significant word means death. To crucify is not to restrain, or curb, or control; it is to kill There is something inside of men, according to

TO CALVARY 69

the teaching of our Lord in Mark, that is most obnoxious and desperately wicked; an immoral fountain from which flows the entire stream of wickedness. This something is dangerous in the highest degree. The teaching of Paul shows that this something, to some extent, remains in those who have been born again, who, although babes in Christ, "are yet carnal." This strange nature which is at enmity with God, fights against and would destroy the new life begotten of God in those who have been regenerated, and have not yet been sanctified; it is the Ishmael of carnality, or the flesh, fighting against the Isaac of the Spirit. It is the Esau of death struggling against the Jacob of the new life in the womb of the regenerated soul. These two principles in man—the Christian man—mark you, battle for the supremacy.

So clearly defined are these inward principles, and so antagonistic are they to each other, that Paul likens them to men at war with each other. In Ephesians 4:22-24, we read: 'That ye put off concerning the former conversation the old man, which is corrupt according to the deceitful lusts; and be renewed in the spirit of your mind; and that ye put on the new man, which after God is created in righteousness, and true holiness." It will be seen at once that the old man represents the "flesh," the carnal nature, and that the new man represents the new life begotten in the soul by the Holy Ghost in regenerating power. This old man and new man, as we have seen in the pen pictures of the flesh life and the Spirit life, are entirely different and in antagonism with each other.

This Scripture is very illuminating. It brings the whole subject into the clear daylight of inspired truth. Here we find the old man full of all sinfulness and corruption spoken of by our Lord in Mark's Gospel, and we find the new man so entirely different, who "after God is created in righteousness and true holiness." What is to be done with this Ishmael of the old life who strives against the Isaac of the new life? What is to be done with this Esau of sin who fights against the Jacob of salvation? Let us turn again to the Apostle for information on this all-important subject: "Knowing this, that our old man is *crucified* with him, that the body of sin might be destroyed, that henceforth we should not serve sin." It is obvious that the crucifixion of the old man, the destruction of the body of sin, the purifying of the hearts of believers, is *not* the work of *regeneration*. It is a work wrought by the baptism with the Holy Ghost subsequent to regeneration. This is the thought in that expressive verse of Charles Wesley's:

"Speak the second time, Be clean,
Take away my inbred sin."

The entire Methodist doctrine of full salvation as taught by John Wesley, the fathers, and founders of Methodism, rests upon the fact of the carnal nature and the teaching of the Holy Scriptures that, notwithstanding men by the regenerating power of the Holy Spirit are born again and become babes in Christ, they are *yet carnal* until the old man is crucified—the body of indwelling sin is destroyed.

Human experience is in perfect harmony with biblical teaching. Christians everywhere have realized that, notwithstanding their regeneration, their love for our Lord, and their full purpose to obey Him, they have been conscious of an inward "prone to wander," a strong tendency toward those things which their intellect and conscience condemn. They also have been conscious of a "hungering and thirsting after righteousness," a longing for a full deliverance from these inward carnal appetites and sinful tendencies. They have sighed, prayed and longed for an application of the blood of our Lord Jesus Christ which cleanseth from all sin, and many tens of thousands have, by the baptism and incoming of the Holy Spirit, realized a full deliverance in the crucifixion of the old man, and the abiding of the Holy Spirit revealing to them the wondrous grace and love of the Lord Jesus in His power to save His people from their sins.

The old man can be crucified, destroyed and cast out, and the Holy Ghost can come in to dwell with the new man, to nurture, to comfort, to guide, and to empower for witnessing and for service.

Having attended to the first principles of the doctrine of Christ let us go on to perfection. Let no Christian be satisfied without the gracious work of the Holy Spirit perfecting him in love. We must not remain in a state of carnal babyhood. God would bring us into man and womanhood in Christ. It is not only our blessed privilege but our bounden duty, to seek with all earnestness the expurgation of the carnal nature, the crucifixion of the old man, the casting out of the entire body of sin that our Lord Jesus who died for us, and whose blood cleanseth us from all sin, may present us to His Father without spot or wrinkle, the trophies of His grace, the sanctified and purchased price of His agony on the cross to redeem us from all sin, and bring us into that holiness without which no man shall see the Lord.

Let me close this message with the words of our Lord, "Blessed are they that do hunger and thirst after righteousness, for they shall be filled." There is an entire consecration, an undoubting faith in Jesus Christ and the Atonement He has made for us, which brings to the hungering and thirsting soul a gracious baptism, an inner purging, a divine fire that consumes all sin and sets up the Kingdom of God within the soul —a kingdom of "righteousness and peace and joy in the Holy Ghost." Amen.

CHAPTER IX

THE MIND OF CHRIST

Text: *"Let this mind be in you, which was also in Christ Jesus."* Phil. 2:5.

I once thought the text required more than was possible for the human, however, as I study the Scriptures I find it is possible, practical and necessary in order to a true Christian life to have in us the mind of Christ.

We must remember that the Apostle has no reference to the intelligence of Christ. In this sense, the mind of Christ is infinite and is quite impossible for the human. If in the study of the text we substitute the word mind with the word disposition we shall more readily grasp the thought the Apostle wishes to convey.

The object of the Christian religion is not only to save men from the consequences of a sinful life, but to save them from sin itself. Redemption is to bring man back to the original purity of the first lovely pair; not that man can ever reach a state in this life that will enable him to hand down to posterity inherent righteousness, but that every fallen man, individually, may be born again —made in Christ a new creature. In a word, the grand object of Christianity is to make sinners by the power of the Atonement as much like Jesus as it is possible for the human to be like the divine. Hence, it is the duty of every Christian to cultivate the disposition and duplicate, as nearly as possible, the character of the Son of God.

The importance of living right cannot possibly by overestimated. The Holy Scriptures have by no means been silent on this subject, but from the Ten Commandments written by the finger of God on Sinai, to our Lord's Sermon on the Mount, line upon line and precept upon precept, the path of duty to our Maker and our fellow man has been marked out with great care and plainness. We have not only had precept but we have also had example. Jesus Christ came into the world, lived and labored among men and, although He was closely watched by those who would have gladly detected in Him the least diescrepancy, there is not on record against Him a single unwise word or improper action. A short time before His ascension He said to His disciples, "I have given you an example."

It is much more difficult to originate than it is to copy or to imitate. Hence, surrounded by many difficulties, we have this advantage: we are to copy the example of Christ. It is the purpose of this sermon to tell in plain and simple language how we may be like Jesus; what it means to have in us the mind of Christ—the disposition and attitude of our Lord.

Much might be said with regard to His obedience to the Father; the patience with which He labored, the zeal with which He spread abroad His teachings, the fortitude with which He suffered, and the general humility that characterized every act of His life; but it is my purpose to speak especially of His obedience to the Father and His mercy toward the sinful, and to urge upon all the importance of following His example and cultivating His disposition in these essential particulars.

Early in His ministry, Jesus said, "I came not down from heaven to do mine own will, but the will of him that sent me." Even before this, when His disciples urged Him to partake of food which they had prepared for Him, He said, "I have meat to eat that ye know not of." When His disciples said, "Hath any man given him aught to eat?" He said, "My meat is to do the will of him that sent me, and to finish his work." When the shadow of the cross was falling over Him and the bloody sweat was bursting from His face, He prayed to the Father saying, "Father, if thou be willing remove this cup from me; nevertheless not my will but thine be done." Paul says, "he humbled himself, and became obedient unto death, even the death of the cross."

We certainly have a wonderful example of obedience here in our divine Master. We will do well to lay this to heart. No degree of faith or service releases the Christian from a careful and strict obedience to the law of God. Obedience is the foundation stone of Christian character. To search the Scriptures, to know His will, to pray and trust for light, strength and guidance to do His will, is the spinal column of Christian manhood and womanhood. Watchful obedience in the little, as well as in the larger things, means much to the soul. No doubt, to live an obedient life would make one peculiar; to appear eccentric, might subject one often to ridicule and sometimes to persecution, but the platform of obedience is built directly under the open windows of promise and blessing.

The faith that falls short of leading a man to search the Scriptures and regulate his life according to their instruction, the laws and the truths laid down in them, is a dead faith. Certainly we are saved by faith, but that faith that fails to bring a soul into conformity with the law and will of God is not a saving faith. We should remember that Jesus has said, "Not every one that saith unto me Lord, Lord, shall enter into the kingdom of heaven, but he that doeth the will of my Father which is in heaven." And as if to impress this important truth indelibly upon our minds, we read the same in the very last chapter of the New Testament, "Blessed are they that do his commandments that they may have right to the Tree of Life and enter in through the gates into the city." The language of Samuel to Saul comes home to many of us laden with bitter reproach, "To obey is better than sacrifice." Shall any intelligent, moral being with all these scriptures looking us squarely in the face, make any pretensions to a religious life, and yet habitually and wilfully violate the laws of God legislated for the just, equal and happy regulation of human society and our attitude of humble and constant obedience to our heavenly Father? It were better to make no pretension to religion than to trifle with God.

I now call attnetion to the attitude of our Lord to sinners. His mission in the world was truly a mission of mercy. Jesus came to seek and to save the lost. This was by no means an easy task. Nothing but infinite mercy could have led Him to undertake the solution of the great problem of sin. It seems that in order to save men, He must hunt them up, search them out, and come into close contact with them. In tears and sweat and blood, He wrought out and announced to the world the plan by which God might be just in the justification of the ungodly. Our Lord Jesus was not merciful in a general sense only, but in a special sense as well. Whoever came to Him that was in any wise turned away without compassion? Upon what would our hope rest but for His compassionate mercy? Mercy is a great central fact in the Atonement. Take it out of the Bible and that good Book has no promise for us. Mercy is the keystone in the arch of the plan of human redemption; remove it and the whole structure will fall into ruin. It is the electric light of Christianity that is illuminating the prodigal's return road to the Father's house. It is the magnet of the Church that must draw the world to Christ.

The Lord Jesus wants us to have within us His mind and practice among our fellowbeings, this same attitude of mercy. It is a pearl of great price. The Christian heart must know how to bear and forbear, how to forgive those who sin against us, how to follow up and seek to save the lost, how to bless and help the unworthy, how to support the weak, to be patient toward the feeble-minded, to give succor and assistance to the unworthy, to hold on, to pray for, and to love those who backslide again and again. Jesus taught us this, Jesus practiced this. This has been the attitude of Jesus toward us in the past. Can we who are so dependent upon the mercy of God refuse mercy to the objects of His love? Shall we not pray earnestly that our Lord Christ may put His mind in us? May He, by the Holy Ghost, work in us His own disposition of obedience toward the Father and compassion toward our fellowbeings so that we shall follow with untiring feet the lost sheep, lift up the fallen and bear the burdens of the weak? Let us be careful to cultivate in ourselves this quality and disposition of our great Exemplar that will lead us to feed the hungry, clothe the naked, forgive the erring, throw the veil of charity over the faults of our brethren and sisters, and pray for the salvation of our enemies.

Shakespeare wrote almost like one inspired when he penned those immortal words:
"The quality of mercy is not strained;
It droppeth like the gentle rain from heaven
Upon the place beneath. 'Tis twice blest,
It blesses him who gives and him who takes.
'Tis mightiest in the mighty,
It better becomes the throned monarch than his

crown.
'Tis an attribute of God Himself, and earthly power
Doth show likest God when mercy seasons justice."

O, that such divine life may be wrought in us by the Holy Ghost that we shall go forth into life filled with the Spirit of obedience to our God and mercy toward all our fellowbeings.

We must keep in mind the fact that God's great objective is the development of genuine Christian character. He desires to fix men so they can stand all the tests and never become unfixed. Salvation is by faith; regeneration is a powerful act of the Holy Ghost, but it is an initiation into a new life, an introduction into a new spiritual world. It is the beginning of a succession of processes, building and development into sainthood, into strength and preparation for service, into fitness for heaven.

The wheat must pass under flail, in order to separation from the straw and chaff; the gold must go through the fire if you would purify it and bring it into service. It is so in the development of Christian character. Perhaps all of us are ready to say, "Let me die the death of the righteous," but are we willing to pass through the processes that purge out all impurity, that takes away every passion, that brings strength out of weakness, wisdom out of ignorance, patience out of petulancy, destroys resentment and pride, and fills us with the spirit of humility and forgiveness.

CHAPTER X

DEVELOPMENT OF CHRISTIAN CHARACTER

Text: *"As an eagle stirreth up her nest, fluttereth over her young, spreadeth abroad her wings; so the Lord alone did lead him, and there was no strange god with him."* Deut. 32:11, 12.

The text is taken from a song of Moses. The time of his departure was at hand; he was full of solicitude for his people, and in this song he reminds them of the gracious deliverance, care and guidance of God. The song abounds in figures; the text is one of the most beautiful and suggestive. He is singing of God's dealings with Jacob, who represents Israel. Through these figures he is conveying to the people ideas of God and His method of directing, developing and strengthening character.

There are auspicious moments in the lives of men, times when great issues hang on a word, a step, a decision, turning points that seal destiny. This was true of Moses when he chose to "suffer affliction with the people of God, rather than to enjoy the pleasures of sin for a season." When he preferred, with a shepherd's crook, to guide a few sheep in the mountains rather than wield a

TO CALVARY

scepter over a nation. It was true of Jacob, when he wrestled with a stranger and mighty Being through the night crying out, "I will not let thee go except thou bless me."

This was true of the persecutor Saul, when a great light shone about him, and he must make his choice to continue his persecution, or to surrender himself and become a chosen vessel of the Lord. Abraham reached a climax in his history when he built his altar, bound Isaac, laid him upon it and lifted the sacrificial knife to take the life of him who was dearest of all things, and heard the voice of God staying his hand, and stood forth crowned forever as the "father of the faithful."

In some way these times come to all of us, times of decision, times of consecration, times when ladders lead up to heaven; when our dearest Isaacs must be bound and laid upon the altar of sacrifice, times when men come to the forks of the road and turn their feet into the paths of holiness and walk in the light, or into the paths of selfishness and grope in darkness.

There is no such thing as a development of strong, holy character without sore trial, bitter testing, severe temptation and positive decision. Where there are mountains there must be valleys. If we would climb up to the mountains of transfiguration we must pass through the dark valleys of humiliation, surrender, death to self, and consecration to our Lord. If we would stand upon the mountain peaks of spiritual victory we must be willing, before such elevation, to descend deep into the valley of death to self, of a crucifixion which eliminates from our nature all carnal love, and brings into our hearts by the power of the Holy Spirit, the love of God.

This way of death to self, to the incoming of the divine nature, at times, would seem impossible, but we must not turn back. Heaven is our great objective; eternity lies out before us. We are transacting business for an unending existence. We can afford to pay a great price for there is a great prize. Sad to say, many turn back and die in the valley and shadows, but those who press forward, as they approach the summits of grace and love, may enter clouds, may become discouraged, may feel that they have reached the highest heights possible to the human, but there are peaks that shoot into the sunlight far above the clouds. Shall we climb them upon our knees? What brightness, what warmth, what purity of atmosphere, what select company! The multitudes have stopped far below; the world with its clamor and falsehood, pomp and tinsel, seems so far away and heaven so very near.

There are high peaks along the mountain range of religious experience, and God invites us there. Not only so, but in infinite love He comes to us with those influences and tests that would break our souls loose from the world and its littleness, and lift us upon the wings of His power into the high altitudes of faith and life and light.

TO CALVARY 83

This is the thought in the text: The eagle delights to build its nest amid the rugged crags of the highest mountain; the nest is made of sticks and twigs. When the eaglets have grown to age and strength sufficient to fly the mother bird insists that they shall leave their nest, and the crag upon which they have perched and plunge out into the air. The young birds hesitate; their wings have not been tested, and the mother bird tears away the sticks and twigs of which the nest is constructed; she determines to give her young ones comfort and repose no longer; they must learn to fly, seek the prey, and support themselves. If the mother bird permitted her young to remain too long in its nest, the muscles of the wings might eventually become so hardened that they never could be used for flight; so she refuses longer to supply her young with food, and she stirreth up her nest, drives them out of their comfort, gives them rest no longer, because continued rest would disqualify them for the high delights of flight. She destroys their place of abode in order that they may seek something far better. When the young bird is forced off the edge of the precipice, and flutters about with its wings unaccustomed to flight, the mother bird will not permit it to fall, but finally diving beneath she catches her young upon her wings and bears it to a place of safety. It is thus that what may seem cruel to the young bird, is really the means of instruction and help until directly it spreads its wings in graceful strength and sails away into the blue dome of heaven.

This is the prophet's figure of God's method with the souls of men. There is an infancy in religious experience; a time when God shelters with great care the little ones in His kingdom; He lets them lie in the nest of comfort and ease while He protests them from the encroachments of the enemy. But there comes a time when they must arouse themselves; they must be up and out and doing something for Christ and humanity; a time for great faith and zealous action. Not infrequently God is compelled in the development of Christian character, to break up the nest in which His children are disposed to rest, to find comfort and contentment. There are countless Christians who can point to experiences that tried their souls; losses that they cannot explain, sorrows that, for the time, tempted them to believe that God cared nothing for their souls; but later on they have come to realize that God was breaking up their nest in order to lead them on to a higher and better state of grace; to bring them into a stronger faith, a deeper experience of divine love, and a service far more active and fruitful than they had once believed possible.

God in mercy plucks away the thing to which we cling in order that our aching hearts may seek better things, and our empty hands may lay hold on eternal things. In the progress of our souls upward, He makes our stopping places so uncom-

TO CALVARY

fortable that we are bound to move out and on. At times He appears to leave us alone to struggle; our strength gives way, we sink down, it appears that our all is lost; our sufferings are unbearable, the wings of our faith seem to be exhausted, the storm beats upon us, and then it is that He comes beneath us and bears us aloft and brings us into a profound sense of our utter dependence upon Him, and that His love and presence mean infinitely more to us than the things to which we once clung; our loss has been our gain.

I am not coming to you in this exhortation with the lullaby words of a mother to her infant, but with the shout of a captain to his soldiers in battle. I would be almost harsh in voice and startling in statement. I would warn you to expect that if God loves you He will pluck away the decaying sticks and twigs on which you rest, that you get out and go up to higher peaks. Satisfied, contented! No, no, out, up, on and on to higher heights until your faith in God shall be like the wings of the eagle in the air. What room, what light, what purity; the world is far below; it sinks away, its fields become garden spots, its great rivers are but threads, its mountains molehills, its noise is hushed; it is like a distant star; it is out of sight. There is music, there is strange fragrance in the air; there is great buoyancy that bears us on; there is a new light, there is a city; it flashes in gold and sparkles in diamonds. Its walls are jasper; it is the New Jerusalem.

CHAPTER XI

GOD'S PLAN FOR A REVIVAL

Text: *"And Samuel spake unto all the house of Israel, saying, If ye do return to the Lord with all your hearts, then put away the strange gods and Ashtaroth from among you, and prepare your hearts unto the Lord, and serve him only; and he will deliver you out of the hand of the Philistines."* 1 Sam. 7:3.

We must have a revival or a revolution. We have not at the present time enough true spiritual salt to permeate and save this nation. There must be a great spiritual awakening or, the decay of morals, the increase of selfishness, and finally, a tremendous social upheaval. The sea of human life is seething with counter current; the billows of prejudice and passion are rolling high. The conflict between capital and labor, the skeptical teaching in seats of learning, the uncertain sound in pulpits, the worldliness crowding into the churches, the immodesty and lewdness thrusting itself upon society, the widespread looseness of family government, the recklessness in the expenditure of money and pleasure seeking among the rising generation, the boldness of the criminal classes, the mob spirit breaking out in all parts of the nation, with all the counter currents of dissatisfaction and unrest among the masses of the people have produced a tempest in this nation that can only be calmed and put at rest by the authoritative voice of the divine Master. Hence, the statement in the beginning of this discourse—we must have a revival or we shall have a revolution. There must be a widespread and deep spiritual awakening in this nation, calling men back to faith in the Bible as the word of God, and obedience to that word, and trust in Jesus Christ for salvation, the cultivation and practice of His teaching under the leadership and empowering of the Holy Spirit in every-day life. or growing worse, our nation on a moral downgrade, will plunge into some tremendous catastrophe of ruin.

The feeling is widespread among thoughtful people everywhere, that nothing short of a great revival of Bible religion can meet the emergencies of the hour. This is not only true with reference to religious teachers, but business men in the wider realms of commercialism and large vision in material matters, are beginning to realize that in order to preserve the foundations of society, maintain commercial integrity and keep order among the masses of humanity, there must be a turning back to faith and obedience to the teaching of the Ten Commandments and the Sermon on the Mount. Hence, intelligent selfishness is pleading for a religious awakening that will insure national progress and the safety of investments and business enterprises.

Men are awakening to the fact that to forget

God is to invite ruin; that "Righteousness exalteth a nation, but sin is a reproach to any people." They are coming to appreciate the exhortation of King David to Israel when he stood up and delivered to them his last great address: "Now therefore in the sight of all Israel the congregation of the Lord, and in the audience of our God, keep and seek for all the commandments of the Lord your God: that ye may possess this good land, and leave it for an inheritance for your children after you forever." 1 Chron. 28:8.

The multitudes are not thinking of God, of the danger of sin and the wickedness of it. The multitudes are seeking after money and pleasure. They are kindling to brighter burning the maddening flames of covetous and lustful desires for the temporal things that perish. They have forgotten God, but serious men and women, everywhere, in all walks and classes of life, are coming to a union of opinion and oneness of conclusion that the only possible remedy for existing conditions is a deep, widespread revival of Bible religion.

Many preachers have undertaken to fill the empty pews of their churches by installing moving pictures. The crowds have come to attend the shows but have not remained to pray. In many places they have turned churches into social centers; there have been feasts and carousals but there was not salt to save and sanctify the gay and thoughtless throngs who desecrated the temples of the Lord by making them houses of carnival and amusement. Many things have been suggested as remedies for the untoward situation; it has been proposed that we have a widespread revival of religion, "Without tears and with no shouting at all." Many people have been brought into the church by one means and another, persuasions, decisions, and professions without the deep conviction wrought in the sinner's soul by the truth of God and the regenerating power of the Holy Ghost. There can be no method that will lead more certainly to the final analysis of the church, the undermining and destroying of Christianity, than the bringing of unregenerated masses of people into the church.

If we are to have a revival that will save the people, permeate the whole moral atmosphere, sanctify the home, introduce the spirit of integrity and honesty into commerce, produce civic righteousness and elevate the ideals of the people, and make firm the foundations of our great republic, such a rival must bring men out of the kingdom of darkness into the kingdom of light; it must change the heart of the individual; men must seek and find the regenerating power of the Holy Ghost; they must become in Christ new creatures.

Such a revival as is here indicated is quite possible. There are those who try to convince us that times have changed, that we are living in a new era of history; that men must be approached from a different angle, that education can take the place of regeneration, that culture and human refinement must be substituted for the sanctifying power of Jesus' blood. All of this is shallow cant; every word of it in contradiction of divine truth and the great facts in human experience. God never changes. He is the same ysterday, today, and forever. Human nature is the same. Customs may change, discoveries in the field of science may be made, but these things do not affect the heart; the natural heart of man remains desperatey wicked. Jesus Christ stands in the midst of the age and delcares, "Except ye be born again ye cannot see the Kingdom of God."

If we have entered upon a new era of history we have brought over into it all the sins of the past era intensified. There never was more crime in the nation than at the present time. Sabbath desecration is fearfully on the increase; modesty of dress on the streets, in the house of God, and in all public places is such an outrage against decency that the editors of secular papers are expressing surprise and disapproval; women's clubs are registering their protest; devout ministers are lifting up their voices in rebuke; cartoonists are using their stencils in ridicule, and people are asking, when shall we reach the limit in the immodest apparel of our American womanhood? There is a dance craze throughout the nation, and the lewd embrace and improper contact of the sexes in the dance halls and hotel ballrooms are of the most appalling and shocking character. The theater and moving picture are absolutely reeking with licentiousness and sowing broadcast among the multitudes of young people who crowd them, the seed that will bring forth a harvest of unchastity that will head up in divorces, broken homes, wrecked families and blasted lives. If we are living in a new age, there has been brought over into it all the sinfulness and wickedness of the old age, intensified and quickened with a tenacity and aggressive boldness unknown before in the history of the American people. The obstacles which stand in the way of revivals of religion are not a new era, a change in God, or His methods of dealing with men; a change in human nature, or the needs of the soul of man; but the difficulty is in the perverseness of man and his effort to substitute notions and plans of his own in the place of the will and word of God.

Isaiah expresses the difficulty very clearly when he says, "Behold the Lord's hand is not shortened, that it cannot save; neither his ear heavy, that he cannot hear: But your iniquities have separated between you and your God, and your sins have hid his face from you, that he will not hear. For your hands are defiled with blood, and your fingers with iniquity; your lips have spoken lies, your tongues have uttered perverseness."

If we are to save this nation from revolution, if we are to preserve the church from woeful backsliding and salt modern society with the teachings and the spirit of the religion of Jesus Christ, if we are to preserve the integrity of the home, maintain parental government, train the rising generation to obedience, the fear of God and righteous living; in a word, if this great nation is to abide in its integrity and continue to march at the head of the column of the progress of the world, and send forth spiritual awakening, a genuine religious revival, we had just as well turn now to the Bible, turn away from all human inventions and substitutes and find in the word of God the true pattern and safe direction for the means to be used to secure the end so greatly needed and so much desired.

Our text offers a solution to the whole problem. It gives us a key that will unlock the situation and lead out into the highway over which we may march to certain and glorious victory. Following the word of God we cannot fail. David strikes the keynote in the 81st Psalm when he says, "But my people would not hearken to my voice; and Israel would none of me. So I gave them up to their own hearts' lust: and they walked in their own counsels. O, that my people had hearkened unto me, and Israel had walked in my ways! I should soon have subdued their enemies, and turned my hand against their adversaries. The haters of the Lord should have submitted themselves unto him."

We see here that the obedience of God's people would have brought the haters of the Lord to submission and obedience to Him. A holy church walking in harmony with the divine will and commandments, filled with the Spirit-breathing love of Christ, will bring about spiritual awakening and outpourings of power which will subdue the wicked, bring them to repentance and obedience before God. But let us come closer to this text and note carefully God's plan for a revival and the gracious results when that plan is carried out.

Israel had sinned; sin had brought separation from God, and separation from God had brought calamities thick and fast. The armies of Israel were being defeated; the Ark of the Lord had been captured. Eli, the backslidden and easygoing priest, under whose lax guidance Israel had drifted into sin, had heard the rebuke of the Lord and had fallen dead when he heard of the capture of the Ark. The Philistines had found the Ark a curse to them; the Ark was of no avail to any people who did not worship the God of the Ark and keep the covenant which was contained therein. The mere emblems of our religion are worth nothing, if we cease to worship God in spirit and in truth. The altars of the church may become a curse if we desecrate those altars with broken vows, and the very house of God may become a snare if we transform it into a place of amusement, instead of a place to learn the duties of the Christian life, to worship and to pray.

For twenty years the Ark of the Lord had

been absent from the central place of worship. It has been kept in Kirjath-jearim, but now there appeared some very hopeful indications. The inspired record says, "All the house of Israel lamented after the Lord." This was indeed encouraging. When men begin to long after God their sins which separate them from Him become hateful. Samuel, noting this spirit of longing among the people, seized the opportunity to break in upon them with the text. Let us repeat it here: "And Samuel spoke unto all the house of Israel, saying, if ye do return unto the Lord with all your hearts, then put away the strange gods and Ashtaroth from among you and prepare your hearts unto the Lord, and serve him only: and he will deliver you out of the hand of the Philistines."

We find the direction of Samuel very clear and positive. The inspired writer tells us that the people obeyed; they put away their idols; they turned wholly to the Lord, and Samuel gathered Israel to Mizpeh and prayed to the Lord for them. The people fasted and prayed and said, "We have sinned against the Lord." The Philistines heard of the gathering and prayers of the Israelites and went up to destroy them; the people were in great distress and plead with Samuel, saying, "Cease not to cry unto the Lord our God for us, that he will save us out of the hand of the Philistines." Then Samuel offered a young lamb as a burnt-offering and continued his prayers for Israel. As Samuel was offering the lamb and pouring out his prayers, "The Philistines drew near to battle against Israel;" and "The Lord thundered on that day upon the Philistines, and discomfitted them; and they were smitten before Israel. Then the Israelites pursued them and smote them, and Samuel set up an Ebenezer stone, saying, Hitherto hath the Lord helped us."

This was a genuine revival. Let us note the steps. First of all, the people, "Lamented after the Lord." They realized their sinfulness; they longed for the restoration of the Ark, for communion and comfort. They applied to their religious teachers for help and guidance. Fortunately, Samuel was not a compromiser. It never occurred to him to suggest human inventions to take the place of the divine plan. God only was able to bring deliverance, restoration and blessing.

Samuel called upon the people to forsake their sins; to put away their strange gods. "They must prepare their hearts unto the Lord, and serve him only." All idols must be cast away and God must have absolute authority. The Israelites obeyed the commandment of Samuel, and then gave themselves to confession, repentance and prayer. At this juncture they met with a great opposition. The Philistines became uneasy and set themselves to break in upon these revival processes. The backslidden people were in an agony of fear and plead for help from God.

Samuel took a young lamb and offered it in burnt-offering. There must be an atonement made for sin. Now, that the Israelites have "Lamented after him," obeyed the voice of His servant, "Put away their strange gods," confessed their sins, given themselves to fasting and prayer, and Samuel offers up the atoning lamb, God comes upon the scene. The Philistines have drawn near to battle; they little realize that they are about to have to contend with the Almighty. The artillery of heaven broke loose upon them; God thundered with a great thunder upon the Philistines. This was no ordinary thunder; it was the voice of the Almighty in crashing wrath against the enemies of His repentant and praying people.

The Philistines understood that this was not common thunder for a shower of rain, but that the Almighty was speaking to them in the boom of His indignation. They were filled with fear and fled for their lives. God can speak to men so that they recognize His voice. There is an inner ear to the human soul that can detect the tone of the supernatural, that quakes and quails before the voice of the Almighty. No man, or army of men, can march up against the artillery of the skies when God thunders in His indignation against their sins and in the defense of His people.

Here we have the spiritual plan of a revival. The church should lament after God, long for Him, desire to feel the power and glory of His presence. She should listen with attentive ear to

TO CALVARY   97

the voice of His ministry, and, O, how important that that ministry be faithful. She should be obedient and purge herself from sin. She needs to fast, confess, and pray and remember the atonement made by the Lamb of God in the agonies of Calvary, and then she may expect God to come upon the scene in His supernatural power.

We ought not to expect a widespread revival from the Lord while we keep in our college and university chairs men who deny the inspiration of the Scriptures and who destroy the faith of the students who are under them for instruction. If Protestantism of these United States wants a mighty spiritual awakening and a great blessing from God; let her have the honesty, the candor and the courage to remove all destructive critics from her theological seminaries. Let her speak with no uncertain sound to those ministers who make light of her fundamental doctrines, and those new theology men who are introducing all sorts of human philosophies and dangerous heresies among the people. Let her purge her universities, her theological seminaries and her pulpits of the priests of Balaam, of her idol worshippers. Let her have a holy courage and zeal for God that will not hesitate to cut off her right hand and pluck out her right eye, if need be. Let her reverence and respect true piety, rather than wealth, and loyalty to the Bible, rather than those smart fellows who are discounting Moses, St. Paul, and worse still, the teaching and authority of the Lord Jesus Christ.

If Protestantism wants a revival let her ministry preach mightily against the wickedness of our times. Let them in holy fearlessness denounce the immodest dress, the lewd dance, the impure theater, the vices of the card table, the wicked lusts and high tide of worldliness on every hand. If she would have God come upon her with a great spiritual awakening, let them pitch their moving picture machines into a dump heap, tear the theatrical platforms from the sanctuary of the Lord, clear out their basketball teams from God's house, and give herself to repentance, to fasting, and to prayer.

Let us be done with all the shallow talk about new methods and unscriptural substitutes for the religion of the Lord Jesus. Let us say less about *decisions* and more about repentance. Let us say less about *confessions* of Christ and more about pardoning mercy and regenerating grace. Let our ministry have a holy courage to warn the people in harmony with the plain teaching of our Lord Jesus, that those who live and die in their sins will wake up in the fires of eternal torment. However, the Philistines may come against us, let us be true to God and His word, rally around the cross in prayer until God comes upon the scene with the thunder of His power. God can rebuke the destructive critics, the false teachers, the movie mongers, the church theatricals, the gaudy, godless gang in their pageants and plays. They can no more stand the thunderings of the Almighty than the heathen Philistines. We need a revival beginning in deep longings after God, followed up with repentance, confession, fasting and prayer, and climaxed by the manifestation of the divine presence, by the thunder of God's indignation against sin, by the glorious manifestation of the Holy Ghost in the salvation of the people.

Nothing can meet the emergency of the times except such revival as is here indicated. Any sort of human schemes and enticements to bring impenitent and unregenerated people into the church is only to burden the church with hindering weights and sink her deeper into backsliding and worldliness. We must have a revival or we shall have a revolution. The great multitudes of discontented and restless people of this nation must be salted with the pure gospel of Jesus, must be saved by the power of the Holy Spirit, or confusion will be worse confused, bitter prejudices will continue to increase; there will be class hatred, social upheaval, blood and fire.

When a people trample upon God's holy Word, reject His Son, refuse His mercy and grieve His Spirit away from them they become self-destructive; there is no need for the fearful judgments of the Lord to be visited upon them. The most fearful judgment that can fall upon a people is for God to withdraw Himself, to simply leave them alone, and they will rise in wrath against each other, pluck the keystone from the arch of civilization and let the whole social fabric come crashing down upon them.

Shall we have a revival? Will the ministry plead with the people and warn them? Can the Church of America be brought to lament after the Lord? Will we come to fasting and prayer and confession of sins? Will we turn away from all subterfuges and sweep away the miserable substitutes for the gospel of Christ and the atonement of Christ? Shall we gather about His pierced feet in worship and faith and prayer until our God shall come into our midst in the glory of His power, rebuking the Philistines of sin, putting to rout the enemies of truth and righteousness? Then will He pour out His Spirit upon His Church, and bring by the regenerating power of the Holy Spirit, multitudes of sinners into the kingdom, sanctifying His people with the blood of Jesus, filling them with the Holy Ghost and making them nursing fathers and mothers in Israel to develop the new-born babes in the kingdom into men and women in Christ. Then, indeed, we could set up our Ebenezer stone and shouting around it could declare like Samuel of old, "Hitherto hath the Lord helped us."

CHAPTER XII

THE ARTILLERY OF HEAVEN

Text: *"The Lord thundered with a great thunder on that day upon the Philistines, and discomfited them; and they were smitten before Israel."*—1 Sam. 7:10.

Judge Samuel was one of the greatest and best men of his times. No man in the early days of Israel in the land of Canaan was more faithful to his God and his people. He was a judge in the highest and best sense, entirely impartial and beyond the probability of being influenced by praise, abuse, bribe, or any selfish motive. He could not be induced to render a biased or unjust verdict. He was an example to be emulated by all judges in all countries through all ages. An unjust or impartial judge, who can be frightened, bribed, or led to render an unjust decision, out of harmony with the written law and the spirit of justice, is the most corrupt and despicable of men. He destroys the foundation of equity, makes law void, and lifts the floodgates of wrong and crime.

Judge Samuel had an excellent background. He was born in answer to prayer, coupled with a promise. His mother, Hannah, was devout and godly; she longed for a son, and offered this prayer: "Give unto thine handmaiden a man child, then will I give unto the Lord all the days of his life." This was the beginning of a great, godly man, consecrated before birth. There was a definite understanding between God and Hannah that Samuel should belong to the Lord. How fortunate was Samuel to have such a mother.

Hannah kept her promise and when little Samuel was weaned she took him to Shiloh and left him with the priest of the Lord; and "the child Samual grew, and was in favor with the Lord, and also with men." No man ever got a better start in life than this great judge of Israel. We can conceive of nothing more fortunate for a child than that it should be born of a godly mother in answer to prayer, and at the same time, definitely consecrated to God.

This humble woman, Hannah, was accomplishing far more for her country than she knew, when she prayed for the child and promised him to the Lord. How fortunate for Israel that some birth control expert did not get the notion into Hannah's head that she would have much larger liberty and be able to render better service to society if she were not cumbered with child-bearing. It would have been fortunate for this nation of ours, and the times in which we are living, if quite a number of our present leaders in the various fields of activity throughout the land, had been born in answer to prayer, and consecrated to God from their birth.

Samuel came to maturity at a time when Israel was in sore need of just such a man. It is always so. Every nation, state, city, or community is al-

TO CALVARY

ways in need of a man of God; a man of pure soul, clear mind, integrity, strength to resist evil, of high purpose, who has a profound reverence for his God and stands as a Gibraltar for justice, righteousness, and everything that is best for his fellowmen. Hannah could not have anticipated all that was embraced in her prayer and promise. She took the chance, prayed, promised, trusted the Lord, believed; Samuel comes along, and when Israel was in great distress, and in danger of extermination, Samuel comes upon the scene girded with power, and illuminated with divine wisdom.

Come to think of it, how unfortunate it would have been for the history of the world, if a certain group of mothers had become so broadminded, up to date, progressive and so deeply interested in public welfare and the uplift of society, that they determined they would not become cumbered with the bearing and rearing of children, but would devote their energies to the general welfare. Take for instance, the mother of Moses, Joshua, John the Baptist, St. Paul, Martin Luther, John Wesley, Bishop Asbury, Bishop Phillips Brooks, Shakespeare, Longfellow, George Washington, Abraham Lincoln, Dwight L. Moody, Bishop Marvin, Bishop Joyce, and a host of others; what a vast gap it would have left in human history, if the mothers of these leaders, and guides of the people, for any reason, had refused to give them birth and training for the great work God had for them in the world.

Judge Samuel came into action at a very important period in the history of Israel. The priest, Eli, was a very soft sort of old man. He held a loose reign of government; his sons *were shockingly corrupt*. Results: Israel was fearfully backslidden, which is always true of the church when we have a soft priesthood, a timid, easy-going ministry under the dictation of a backslidden church, rather than mighty men in the sacred desk smiting formalism, deadness and wickedness with the sword of the Spirit.

The Lord spoke very positively to Eli with reference to himself and sons, saying, "Them that honor me, I will honor, and they that despise me shall be lightly esteemed." Furthermore, He assured the poor old worthless priest that "I will raise me up a faithful priest who shall do according to that within my heart and in my mind; and he shall walk before mine anointed forever." We discover here that God has a place for, and the world has a need for the sons of mothers who pray, promise, nurture, and train children in the fear of God, and consecrate them to His service.

The Philistines were constant enemies of the Levites and Israel was in a fearfully backslidden state when they went to war against their enemies. The Philistines so completely vanquished them that their army was put to rout, and the ark of God was captured. It was a shocking calamity. When poor old Eli heard it, he fell backward from his seat and broke his neck. A miserable death for a priest who had utterly failed in the discharge of his duty. His sons were slain; it looked as if Israel was doomed to destruction, and doubtless would have been if a certain pious mother had not prayed for a son, promised him to the Lord, and kept her promise. It is wonderful what a good woman and God can do for a nation in time of distress and disaster. Personally, I cannot have much hope for a nation without devout, and godly mothers who pray, promise, train and believe as they bring their children up in the nurture of the Lord. A beer-drinking, cigarette-smoking, bridge-playing motherhood cannot produce the man and womanhood that will preserve the integrity of our republic and go forward with a progressive civilization.

The situation was most discouraging. Israel had been put to flight. The ark of God is captured and held by the triumphant forces of the ancient modernists, or the idolatrous Philistines. A mere handful have rallied to come back to the field of battle. They are utterly discouraged; they are largely outnumbered by a victorious foe, and it appears that they are God-forsaken. In this crisis Judge Samuel comes upon the scene. Listen to what he has to say to his trembling and defeated people: "And Samuel spake unto all the house of Israel, saying, if ye do return unto the Lord with all your hearts, then put away the strange gods, and Ashtaroth from among you, and prepare your hearts unto the Lord, and serve him only; and he will deliver you out of the hands of the Philistines."

This was a sweeping demand on the part of Samuel, but there was in him a divine life; his word was with authority and power. Trembling Israel pledged a clean sweep of all of her idolatries. They saw the extremity into which their sins had brought them; that was most fortunate. Sometimes people refuse to see their sins; they resent rebuke, they laugh at the warning and entreaty of the prophets of the Lord. They degrade the very church of God; they spurn the message of warning. Not so with Israel at this time when they trembled before the assembled host that seems to mean their destruction. The record says, "And the children of Israel said unto Samuel, cease not to cry unto the Lord our God for us, that he will save us out of the hands of the Philistines."

It is most fortunate when people in their sins and distresses are willing to hear the command, admonitions and instructions of the prophets of the Lord. At such time, a man of real courage is necessary, a man who, without evasion, will uncover, rebuke sin, and lay down the terms of deliverance and salvation; a man who, all the while, in his Lord, can offer effectual and prevailing prayer.

A sacrifice for sins was necessary; so Samuel took an innocent lamb and offered it up to God, calling for mercy upon his people; and the rec-

TO CALVARY 107

ord says, "And Samuel cried unto the Lord for Israel, and the Lord heard him." Ah, that gives us hope! A sacrifice for sin! A faithful prayer, and an answer from heaven.

Without going further into the story as given in sacred Writ, I am believing that the Philistines will be defeated; I care not how vast their army, how well drilled, how excellently armed, how courageous they may be, and how ready to swoop down upon the Israelites for their destruction, I am believing for Israel, for God and Samuel have come upon the scene; an almighty God and a holy man are powerful re-enforcement.

Finally, we have gotten to our text: "The Lord thundered with a great thunder on that day upon the Philistines, and discomfited them; and they were smitten before Israel." Take notice, my reader, this was not ordinary, growling thunder that jars the rain out of the clouds; that need not frighten any one; but the thunder that day was the resounding crash of heaven's artillery. There was something in that thunder that meant destruction to idolaters. It sounded like the voice of God in battle for righteousness.. There was a strange something in it that made the hearts of the Philistines to quake. They were filled with fear. They threw down their arms in consternation and took to flight. Israel pursued them in glorious victory. There has never been manufactured, even in this age of powerful guns, anything equal to the artillery of heaven. Our God can put a crashing tone into his thunder that will shake the hearts of the wicked until all their pride and strength are shattered and they take to flight.

There is a valuable lesson here, if we would learn it. The way to the defeat of the enemies of righteousness, the way to a revival of spiritual life and power in the Church of God, is for the church to admit her backslidings, to confess her sins, to put away all of her idols, to pledge herself to obedience and faithfulness; to offer up in her prayers, the Lamb of God who taketh away the sin of the world; not only to cry for mercy herself, but to appeal to the prophets of the Lord to cry unto God in her behalf.

The same God who thundered against the Philistines still has the artillery of heaven under His command. He can so direct the crashes of His thunder against sin that the hosts of wickedness will be paralyzed with fear and flee before the onward march of the consecrated hosts of the Israel of God. The days of revivals have not passed, if the Lord's people will repent, if they will turn away from their sins; if they will humble themselves and cry to the Lord for mercy, He will speak in thunder tones of rebuke to the tremendous forces of evil that are in defiance of His law, who trample humanity beneath their feet, who deluge the land with liquor and drunkenness, who work riot in the Church of God, breaking up our homes, driving our young people from the church, and leading them away from truth and righteousness. Our God is more mighty than all the combined forces of the foes of righteousness. If we will adjust ourselves to the divine law and will of God, He will bring the artillery of heaven into action, the thunder of His power will go through the nation; the forces of evil will be broken, and the Church of God will advance to victory.

At this very time we are in dire need of men of the character and spirit of Samuel; of just, holy, fearless, praying men who will rebuke sin with authority and can pray the thunder of God's artillery upon the foes of righteousness. It seems there is a sad lack of such men. Can it be that thirty, forty, or fifty years ago there was a scarcity of Hannahs; that mothers were not praying, consecrating, promising and giving to God sons who would grow up into mighty men able to beat back the forces of evil?

The distressing condition in which we find ourselves today must not hide our eyes from the future. It is our duty to prepare for the future, to see that there are Samuels in the years to come to deliver the children of God from the Philistines of modernism, the liquor traffic, corruption in office, Elis prophesying soft things in pulpits, and the people drifting away until their skeptical enemies shall capture the ark of God and set it up with mockery in the temples of modernism.

We cannot believe that the bridge-playing members of our Protestant churches will be able to produce Samuels for the tomorrows. Sunday golf players will not beget and rear sons who, in the day of calamity, can cry to the Lord and bring deliverance to the nation. There is not a doubt in the mind of this writer, but that one of the greatest needs of the times in which we are living, and the times just ahead of us, is a consecrated, devout, praying motherhood. Elkannah was a very good sort of man, but Hannah, with her prayers and devotion brought forth and consecrated the Samuel who led Israel out of disaster. Give us godly women who sanctify the homes in which they preside with reverence and devotion, whose children are born into the world in answer to prayer, consecrated to God, and our future will be safe. No nation can fail with a consecrated, godly motherhood. No nation can survive with a godless motherhood who encourages drink, fills the atmosphere with tobacco smoke, gathers about the card table, and profanes everything that is sacred and holy. In the economy of human life, there is something so sacred, so close to God, so beautiful and holy in devout and consecrated motherhood, that it is absolutely above all price. It is worth more than all the resources of wealth. It is more powerful than all the armies, navies, and fleets of airships of any nation. A holy womanhood means consecrated and reverential childhood, and by and by, mighty Samuels rise up, stand in the breach, break the powers of the foes of God and humanity, and bring down from heaven the tremendous spiritual forces that will sweep away all the foes of righteousness.

CHAPTER XIII

REJECTED LIGHT

Text: *"In him was life; and the life was the light of men. And the light shineth in darkness; and the darkness comprehended it not."* John 1:4, 5.

These words are found in the introductory to the Gospel by John. They refer to the coming of Christ among men and their failure to recognize Him as the Messiah and Redeemer. This seems one of the strangest and most stupid blunders in all the history of the human race.

The Hebrew prophets had so clearly pointed out the coming of the Lord, and had given such minute details with reference to His character, His conduct, and His ministry and the history unfolding about Him that it would seem almost impossible for these men who had familiarized themselves all their lives with the writings of the prophets to fail to recognize the Christ.

The only way to account for this blindness of the Jews, and their failure to recognize in Jesus the Messiah for whom they had looked and waited so long, is the fact that they were in a fearfully backslidden state. Spiritual things are spiritually discerned. They had only the letter without the spirit of law and prophecy. Jesus said to them, "If ye had known my Father ye would have known me." These Jews knew about God, but they did not know Him. This blindness and failure to recognize Jesus as the promised Messiah and Redeemer of men were not confined entirely to these Jews or to any period in history or any one people. With the progress of history, the growth of the church, the countless multitudes who can witness to the saving power of Jesus, we have in the church today vast multitudes of people who claim to be Bible students, who claim to be fully as pious, even more pious, than the Jews who rejected Jesus and manipulated the influences and directed the course of events which finally brought Him to the Cross, who also deny the Godhead of Christ and His saving power. This is quite common in our day. Multitudes of people in the various churches are quite as slow to receive Jesus Christ as God manifest in the flesh, the only Saviour from sin, as were the Jews to receive Him as the promised Messiah of prophecy and the Redeemer of His people. John very sadly records of the Jews of the time of Christ, "He was in the world, and the world was made by him, and the world knew him not. He came unto his own, and his own received him not." Is this not quite true today? Is Jesus not being rejected as Saviour and Lord by multitudes of professed Christians? The rejecters of Christ today have far greater light than had the Jews. They also have the history and example of those Jews who secured the rejection and crucifixion of Jesus and yet they per-

TO CALVARY 113

sist in denying His Godhead, His miracle-working power and His vicarious suffering and the atonement He made for a lost world upon the Cross.

If the church loses her touch with God, if she becomes busy with the temporal and material things of the Kingdom, if she is engrossed with the prejudice and pride of sectarianism, if she comes to use the holy things of God for selfish motives and for the gratification of the ambitious desires of men, then the church becomes as blind, possibly more blind, to the things of the spiritual kingdom than the world itself.

In the days of Christ on earth certain Roman officers believed in and accepted Him as God's Son and representative on earth, while priests rejected and derided Him, and even the publicans and sinners heard Him gladly, felt the strange and blessed power of His personality and the truths which He preached, while those who were well versed in prophecy and would have been supposed to have received Him gladly, were full of hatred and scorn against Him. The attitude of Pilate, the Roman governor, at the trial of our Lord, was far more generous than the attitude of the chief priest and his adherents.

There is perhaps no blindness which makes it so impossible to discover the truths of salvation as the blindness of religious conceit, ecclesiastical prejudice, and the carnal ambitions of those who would prostitute the church from her true bride-hood to Jesus and use her for the advancement of their own selfish motives and wicked designs.

Great light had shone upon Jerusalem and Judea, but the apostate church was too blind to behold its radiance and beauty. The calamities which followed were unutterable in ruin and horror. No people has ever been subject to more fearful suffering and utter destruction than were those Jews on whom the light had shone, and who rejected that light.

It should be borne in mind that the rejection of light brings darkness; the rejection of divine mercy brings judgment; evil follows close and rapidly on the heels of rejected good. Sodom and Gomorrah rejected mercy and fire rained down upon them. Nineveh repented and was spared and blessed. This is the logic of the Kingdom of heaven. This is in harmony with the eternal fitness of things. Judgments follow close after rejected mercy. Those who refuse the light of heaven must eventually be driven into the darkness of hell.

If you take the back track of history and look deeply into the cause of the calamities that have come upon the earth, the downfall of nations, the breaking up of empires and the destruction of peoples, you will find that sin has been the cause, that men have sought darkness rather than light. They have rejected the truth and chosen falsehood. They have hated holiness and loved iniquity. They have sown to the wind, and as sure as God reigns and His word is true, they have had to reap the whirlwind. When the light of divine love and mercy shines upon men and they reject it, refuse to comprehend, to change their way, to repent of their sins and turn their feet into the paths of repentance, wisdom and mercy, ruin must inevitably follow. It is beyond the power of God to make the wicked happy, to give them peace, to grant them pardon and salvation if they will not repent and change their ways. By and by the fruitless tree must be cut down as a cumberer of the ground. This is true of individuals, of communities, of nations where great light is given and gracious opportunities are offered and special mercies extended and rejected. Fearful judgments follow. Finally, God must deal with men. In the end, there is one of two things that God in the nature of things is compelled to do with the individual and with the nation; He will pardon or He will punish. Those who will not receive life must have death. Those who utterly refuse heaven choose hell.

It is impossible to build an empire so large, to found a nation so strong, to organize armies so complete, to develop commerce so great and to amass riches sufficient to protect and guard yourself, so secure that you may reject the light of heaven, refuse the commandments, counsels and warnings of God and escape His judgments. The highway of history is littered with fallen empires, wrecked nations and ruined cities which have refused divine guidance, refused to listen to the inviting and warning voice of God. Nations and people who have trampled upon divine law, have had their own way with themselves, and have met with inevitable disaster.

It seems hard for humanity to learn the all-important lesson that those who sow the seeds of rebellion against God must reap a harvest of punishment from God. Somehow, men persist in forgetting. By and by they refuse to listen to the voice of the past or to believe its solemn testimony and warning. They say there was no flood; there were no Sodom and Gomorrah; they would like to say there was no Babylonian, Persian, Grecian or Roman empires, but there on your bookshelves are the histories, and yonder on the desolate plains are the ruins which prove that when men and nations refuse the light darkness will inevitably follow. It has ever been so and will ever be so.

Infidels are telling us that the Gospel has failed; that it has been, and is now, insufficient to civilize and lift men out of barbarism, war, confusion and world decay. They should remember that the Gospel has never undertaken or promised to save men who reject it. The Gospel cannot produce a civilization in harmony with the character and teachings of Christ when the vast majority of the civilization deny or entirely ignore the divine origin and saving power of the Gospel.

How different the history of the world would be if men from the days of Abraham, with a fidelity like his, had have learned to obey the commandments of God, believe the promises of God and consecrate to Him those things which they loved best. Suppose the entire Hebrew nation had surrendered to the Lord Jesus as did the Apostle Paul and gone out with a burning zeal to convert the world. Long ago the banner of the cross would have waved over every nation. What would have been the result if all England, all the people of the churches in England in the days of Wesley had joined in sympathy, prayer and zeal in a holy consecration for the evangelization of the British Isles with John and Charles Wesley, Adam Clarke, John Fletcher and Richard Watson? Think of what a center of spiritual influence the British Isles would have become, and how that influence would have penetrated and permeated the great nations of Europe and made impossible the ravage, bloodshed and ruin of the World War.

Had Methodism kept the spirit of McKendree, had the Methodist preachers of this nation, North and South, East and West, been wholly sanctified, filled with the Holy Ghost, and kept the fires of revival burning everywhere, and before the people constant call to an entire consecration and the sanctifying power of the Holy Ghost, we never would have had any civil war. Freedom would have come without bloodshed and the pages of history would glow with the records of the splendid victories of the Cross of Christ and the salvation of untold multitudes who have gone out in darkness. Jesus Christ and His Gospel cannot illuminate the darkened souls of men who refuse to receive Him, who will not comprehend, who persist in sin, in rejection of the truth, and go forward stumbling on in the darkness and pride of their own wicked hearts. Let those who are rejecting the Gospel with its light today make sure they will find darkness tomorrow. There is no darkness so dense, so black, and so eternal, as that which comes to those who will not receive the Bible. Take warning, fellow being, and make haste to receive the Lord, to walk in the light here, and dwell in the eternal light hereafter.

CHAPTER XIV

SEEKING A BRIDE FOR ISAAC

Text: *Thou shalt not take a wife unto my son of the daughters of the Canaanites, among whom I dwell: but thou shalt go to my country, and to my kindred, and take a wife unto my son Isaac.* Gen. 24:3, 4.

Abraham's wife had died; the tent was empty and the men folks were sad. There can hardly be any such vacancy and desolation in a home as that which comes to it when a good wife is taken out by death to come back no more. Abraham bethought himself that Isaac was of marriageable age, and he remembered the promise of God that Isaac was to be the father of a great nation. This being true Isaac's wife must be the mother of the family that was to multiply and grow into a nation; and Abraham knew that it was impossible to have a good family without a good mother, and his heart was set that Isaac should not marry anyone of the mixed breeds about him.

With this thought in mind he called his servant Eleazer, put him under solemn oath to go back to his own country and kindred to find a bride for Isaac, and sent him forth on the delicate and all-important mission of selecting a mother for Israel.

We have often thought of the wisdom of Abraham in this matter. It seems quite impossible to raise a good family without a good mother. We do not know of a single exception to this rule. We have known many instances where excellent families have grown up under the guidance of a devout and godly mother where the father was quite undependable and worthless. We have known drunken fathers with sober families of children, lazy, indolent fathers with industrious and thrifty children, ignorant, easy-going fathers with energetic, intelligent and successful children; but in every such instance this remarkable condition of things was accounted for in the life and character of the mother of the children.

Sometime ago, I was invited to supper by one of the great business men of Columbus, Ohio. I went to his beautiful home and looked with pleasure on his interesting family. In the course of the evening when we were alone, he said to me, "My father was one of the worst drunkards I ever knew, but my mother was one of the most consecrated Christians I ever knew, and she claimed us all with a faith and prayer that would take no denial. There were three brothers of us and several sisters; not one of us boys ever touched a drop of strong drink; we have all been successful men. My sisters all married sober, good men; the secret of our salvation and success all lay wrapped up in the excellent Christian character of a mother who walked before us in humble devotion to Christ and cried to God day and night for the salvation of her children.

One of the great preachers of this country, conversing with me once, fell into a confidential mood and said to me, "My father was a weak, dissolute drunkard, a poor, helpless sort of man, but my mother, a very small woman, pinched with poverty and burdened with many cares, was a strong, brave soul, who gripped the Lord with a strong hand of faith and her children with a strong hand of love. She would never let Him or us go. She was the connecting link that bound us to hope and heaven. We were all sober, and were all saved, all have become useful in the world. I have preached up and down this nation for many years; I have seen ten thousand souls brought to Jesus under my personal ministry and it is all because of the devotion and prayers of my faithful mother. She ruled my boyhood life with a strong hand, chastised me when I needed it, made me obey, led me to Christ and trained me for His service."

I recall in memory, a family; the woman's father was a man of wealth and influence; he tried to dissuade his daughter from marrying a handsome young drunkard; she believed she could reform him, but she failed, and after she had borne him six children and he had treated her with every brutality, she brought her ragged, lean children and broken furniture back to our community. I was a small boy but I shall never forget the sensation that it created. She had gone away young, beautiful, with a handsome little fortune;

she had come back broken, poor and burdened with an almost helpless family. She settled on her father's old farm adjoining that of my grandfather and she and her little children worked together from sun to sun. I remember a remark of a neighbor man whom I heard talking to my grandfather about this woman. He said, "I was over in the woods the other day and Mrs. Blank came out with an ax on her shoulder, drove it into the tree, clasped her hands together and looking up, said: 'O Lord, give me strength to chop this tree down.' She then went to work with a will." He said, "I hurried out of the woods to keep that tree from falling on me."

I remember in my boyhood mind to have thought of God and Mrs. Blank chopping trees, raising wheat, cultivating corn and running the farm. I remember how she prospered, how the children grew, how they were converted, and what useful citizens they became.

It seems that there is something unconquerable and invincible about a good woman; a woman who lives a life of prayer and faith, which couples her on to Omnipotence, can hardly be thwarted in her purpose. She will save her family in spite of a godless husband. She will win out, when to win, seems impossible. She is indeed, the salt of the earth, the light of the world.

I do not believe there is any human power in all the world comparable to that of a consecrated, Christian mother, who has an unswerving faith in

God and an unending love for her offspring. There is no other asset in all the world's wealth equal to that of consecrated motherhood. You may take all the resources of your farming land, your mountains of minerals, your water power, your commerce by land and sea, your manufacturing interests, and your great modern cities, but the richest resource of any country, that which counts for far more than all material wealth, is godly motherhood. What would all things else be worth if we have not a population of intelligent people to develop and enjoy the resources of the earth, and how can we hope for a population of intelligent and law-abiding people if we have not Christian homes, and how can we have Christian homes without consecrated, godly mothers? Their faith and devotion and love are the very foundation of society. Without the godly mother all else must fail. She is more important than your teachers in all your schools, than your legislators in all your halls; she gets far closer to the heart of the life of the coming generation than all of your ministers of the gospel; she is the very spring and fountain from which flows the future weal or woe of the community, the Church and the nation. Give us godly, faithful mothers, who live in harmony with the word of God and train their children to fear, revere and obey the God of the Bible, and we can solve all of our problems, conquer all of our enemies, and safely ride the tempestuous sea of social, commercial, and political life into the port of prosperity, peace and happiness. There is no remedy for the lack of good mothers. You cannot give us schools, churches or civil legislation that will remedy the lack in the young life of the proper training at the knee of a Christian mother. You may take almost any life of a man or woman that has been pre-eminently useful in the world and trace the influences that made it such back to the warm, loving heart of a godly mother. If you mothers fail the school will fail, the Church will fail, the State will fail. The foundations will give way beneath society and inevitably calamity must come to the race. Mothers, do not imagine that your sphere is a small one, or that your work in the world is secondary to that of any one else. Whether you live in palace, two-story, cottage or hut, your opportunities are unlimited; the possibilities of your influence over your children cannot be calculated by our mathematics, or limited by time. The courage, the strength and calmness with which the mighty Lincoln held and saved his nation in the darkest day of her history, all lay in the heart of little Nancy Hanks in yonder log cabin in the woods of old Kentucky.

The great Methodist revival that has swept the world with holy fire and brought its millions out of sin into the eternal city of the skies, was smoldering in the bosom of Susanna Wesley while she nursed her little John upon her faithful breast. A countless host of godly women, who are now at the Master's feet in glory, rise before me. They lived, bore children, prevailed with God, corrected, taught, triumphed, conquered Satan and sin for themselves and their offspring, sent their children forth to do battle for the Lord and have gone home to heaven to rest and rejoice until their loved ones shall come home with their arms full of sheaves, gleaned because of the faithfulness of their mother, to lay at the Master's feet.

CHAPTER XV

THE BAPTISM WITH THE HOLY SPIRIT

Text: *"Ye shall receive power, after that the Holy Ghost is come upon you."* Acts 1:8.

Those religious teachers who oppose the doctrine and experience of entire sanctification, as a work of grace wrought in the heart of the regenerated by a definite baptism with the Holy Spirit, have always had trouble in undertaking to explain the purifying baptism with the Holy Spirit received by the disciples on the day of Pentecost.

Not long since in one of our Sunday school magazines, a Nashville writer, a very beloved brother, tells us that the baptism with the Holy Spirit is not for cleansing, but for witnessing. Of course, he is out of harmony with the testimony of St. Peter who tells us that those who received the baptism on the day of Pentecost experienced the purifying of their hearts.

We can hardly understand why a Christian should object to a purifying blessing, to a gracious act of the Holy Spirit cleansing the heart from all sin. We can think of nothing more desirable than a heart from sin set free. If our brethren of the opposition to the old Wesleyan Methodist doctrine of a definite work of grace subsequent to regeneration, sanctifying their hearts from all sin, admit that the disciples were in a state of justification before Pentecost, they find themselves compelled to fall into harmony with the teachings of those great scholars and saintly men who, under God, brought Methodism into the world.

In order to avoid this conclusion, and get away from sanctification as a work of grace subsequent to regeneration, these brethren have been forced to insist that the disciples were not in a state of justification, therefore, were not saved men up to the day of Pentecost. This line of argument brings them into direct conflict with the teachings of the Scriptures.

I want us to examine the facts and find out the state of the disciples before they received their pentecostal blessing. We shall go to Matthew 10, where we find Christ, "When he had called unto him his twelve disciples, he gave them power against unclean spirits, to cast them out, and to heal all manner of sickness and all manner of disease." Matt. 10:1. We find in His instruction to these disciples that Jesus said, "And as ye go, preach, saying, the kingdom of heaven is at hand. Heal the sick, cleanse the leper, raise the dead, cast out devils; freely ye have received, freely give." Matt. 10:7, 8.

It is strange that any religious teacher could bring himself to believe, and insist, that our Lord Jesus was giving such commandment and commission to a group of unsaved men. We find Him giving this instruction, "And when ye come into an house, salute it. And if the house be worthy, let your peace come upon it: but if it be not worthy, let your peace return to you." Matt. 10:12, 13. We see that according to the statement of our Lord, the disciples had peace, not only for themselves, but a blessed peace that could come into the homes in which they were entertained. "But there is no peace to the wicked, saith my God." Only those in a state of justification can have peace, and in some sense impart it to those who give fellowship and entertainment.

In Luke, tenth chapter, Jesus cautioned His disciples not to rejoice over the good work which they had wrought, and the fact that evil spirits were subject unto them, "But rather rejoice because your names are written in heaven." This is said especially of the "seventy" who went forth, two by two, to preach and to heal. This was quite a while before Pentecost.

Turning to John 14, we find our Lord giving these words of comfort to His disciples: In the 13th chapter He had assured them of the coming separation which gave them deep sorrow. He then comforted them with these words: "If ye love me, keep my commandments. And I will pray the Father, and he shall give you another Comforter, that he may abide with you forever; even the Spirit of truth; whom the world cannot receive, because it seeth him not, neither knoweth him: But ye know him; for he dwelleth with you, and shall be in you." John 14:15-17.

These words from our Lord give us positive proof that the disciples were in a state of salvation. They are told that they know the Holy Spirit, and that He dwelleth with them. We could not desire a clearer statement that they were in a state of salvation, and they were assured of another distinct blessing—the coming of the Holy Spirit, not only to dwell *with* them, but to be *in* them.

Following this thought in John 15, we have Jesus teaching with the vine and branches the very intimate relation between Him and His disciples, and exhorting them thus: "Abide in me, and I in you. As the branch cannot bear fruit of itself, except it abide in the vine; no more can ye, except ye abide in me." He continues: "As the Father hath loved me, so have I loved you, continue ye in my love." Notice the word "continue." They were in the love of Christ and He exhorts them to continue in that blessed relation.

We notice that in His words of consolation our Lord says to His disciples, "But when the Comforter is come, whom I will send unto you from the Father, even the Spirit of truth, which proceedeth from the Father, he shall testify of me: and ye also shall bear witness, because ye have been with me from the beginning." John 15:26, 27.

In John 16th chapter we find our Lord saying to His disciples, "I have yet many things to say unto you, but ye cannot bear them now. Howbeit when he, the Spirit of truth, is come, he will guide you into all truth: for he shall not speak of himself; but he will show you things to come. He shall glorify me: for he shall receive of mine and shall show it unto you." John 16:12-14. This does not seem to be the character of language that Christ would use to unpardoned, unsaved men. There is no utterance of a rebuke against sin. There is no exhortation to repentance. We do not find Him saying to them, "Ye must be born again." Evidently, they had been born again, and our Lord speaks to them as the children of God, comforting their hearts with the assurance of the coming and abiding of the Holy Spirit.

Take the 33rd verse of this 16th chapter, and we have the Lord saying, "These things have I spoken unto you, that in me ye might have peace. In the world ye shall have tribulation: but be of good cheer; I have overcome the world." These are not words of rebuke, or exhortation to a group of unsaved sinners, but they are words of assurance to devout believers.

In the 17th chapter of John we find Jesus offering a fervent prayer, in the first of which He speaks of a relationship between Himself and the eternal Father. In verse 9 He begins to pray for His disciples, saying, "I pray for them; I pray not for the world, but for them which thou hast given me; they are thine. And all mine are thine, and thine are mine, and I am glorified in them." It would seem that this statement should settle controversy on the subject. They were not sinners under condemnation; they were saved men; they belonged to the Father and the Son.

We read further, "While I was with them in the world, I kept them in thy name; those that thou gavest me I have kept, and none of them is lost, but the son of perdition that the Scriptures might be fulfilled." Here we have the positive statement that none of them is lost, present tense. therefore, they were saved, therefore, they were pardoned and in a state of justification. This being true, the gracious work wrought in them on the day of Pentecost was not regeneration, but a sanctifying, purifying, incoming and abiding of the Holy Spirit.

We read further in this 17th chapter, "These things I speak in the world, that they might have my joy fulfilled in themselves. I have given them thy word; and the world hath hated them, because they are not of the world, even as I am not of the world. I pray not that thou shouldest take them out of the world, but that thou shouldest keep them from the evil." The revised version has it "evil one." "They are not of the world, even as I am not of the world. Sanctify them through thy truth; thy word is truth."

The teaching is clear. The disciples were in a regenerated state. Their names were written in the Lamb's book of life. They were not of the world. They were preachers of the truth; they had peace; they had power to cast out evil spirits and heal the sick. Jesus is promising them in this teaching exactly what He reiterated in the first chapter of Acts, immediately before His ascension, where He says, "And, being assembled together with them, commanded them that they should not depart from Jersualem, but wait for the promise of the Father, which, saith he, ye have heard of me." Here He refers to that promise in John 14 where He assures them that if they love Him and keep His commandments, they should have another Comforter to abide with them forever.

Reading on, "For John truly baptized with water; but ye shall be baptized with the Holy Ghost not many days hence." He contiuues, "But ye shall receive power, after that the Holy Ghost is come upon you; and ye shall be witnesses unto me, both in Jerusalem, and in all Judea, and in Samaria, and unto the uttermost part of the earth." These were the last audible words of Jesus to His disciples, immediately after which, He was received up into heaven. The disciples tarried and on the day of Pentecost received the baptism with the Holy Ghost purifying their hearts by faith. And Peter gives us the assurance that this baptism is for all of God's children in these words: "For the promise is unto you, and to your children, and to all that are afar off, even as many as the Lord our God shall call."

It appears that these teachings should bring all of God's children to see that the baptism with the Holy Spirit is not regeneration, but a powerful blessing for the regenerate. We find that, as the disciples went forth that believers were baptized with the Holy Ghost. Had this faith been preserved, this doctrine preached, and the fact understood and proclaimed, that every child of God was entitled to the reception of the Holy Ghost in His cleansing and empowering, we would have had a church separate from sin, cleansed from all the carnal nature, and empowered by the incoming and abiding of the Third Person of the Trinity, and doubtless, long ago, the world would have been evangelized.

We do not mean that every one would have been regenerated, but that the gospel would, doubtless, centuries ago, have been preached to the whole world. The indwelling Spirit would have made the Church a chaste, holy and fruitful Bride; nations would have lived in fellowship; the devastating wars of recent years would not have been fought. Untold millions of immortal souls that have gone out in darkness, would have been saved, and gone into eternal life. The great mistake of the Church has been, not only the neglect of this central Bible truth, but opposition to it. The result has been spiritual paralysis, the delay of world evangelization, and countless evils and wreckage among men.

Why shall not we at this late day turn away from unbelief, and the entire Church of God consecrate itself and open wide its heart for the reception, the cleansing and empowering of the Holy Ghost, the turning back of the tides of sin and wickedness, and the great revival so sorely needed, and that can only come when the Holy Ghost is recognized, received and gives power to the Church of Christ to accomplish its purpose in the salvation of the souls of men.

Why is it that the Church is suffering defeat all along the line of battle? Why is it that the forces of evil are advancing with shouts of triumphant mockery? Why is it that the enemies of God and men are not confounded, overwhelmed with conviction, and saving faith in Christ? The answer is easy—the Church is not properly equipped for the conflict. The one essential for her conquest of the world and her victories over the powers of evil, is the baptism, teaching, leadership and empowering of the Holy Ghost. Let the Church be filled with the Spirit and then she is an invincible, conquering host of God going forward from conquest to victory.

CHAPTER XVI

THE CHRIST OF PROPHECY

Text: *"And beginning at Moses and all the prophets, he expounded unto them in all the scriptures the things concerning himself."*—Luke 24:27.

According to chronology is was something more than four thousand years from the fall of Adam to the crucifixion of Christ; but from the time of that fatal fall in the Garden of Eden, to that tragic crucifixion on the hill of Calvary, there was strung all along the highway of human history a line of prophecy bringing to sinful men the promise of a Redeemer. The first hint of hope to fallen man is given in the promise that "The seed of the woman should bruise the serpent's head." From Mount Moriah Abraham saw the day of Christ and was glad.

I think there are three facts that will be readily admitted by all devout students of the Scriptures. First, the ancient Hebrew prophets saw in their visions and promised in their messages a coming Redeemer and King. The harmony of the predictions with reference to this coming Messiah is most remarkable. The casual reader will soon understand that the different prophets, living in various countries, and at periods of time wide apart, beheld afar, and spoke of the same Christ. There are no contradictions or disagreements among the prophets concerning the world's Messiah. Their combined drawings make a complete picture of the Christ. Unite their writings and you have the earthly history of our Lord long before He was born in Bethlehem.

Second, Jesus Christ claimed to be the promised Messiah. He spoke of Himself as the Redeemer of whom the prophets had spoken through the centuries. He never hesitated to identify Himself as the sent of God in fulfillment of the prophecies of the ancient seers of Israel. He held to this claim when He knew it meant crucifixion. He testified to the same after His resurrection. In His birth, life, teaching, sufferings and humiliation, His death, with the incidents connected therewith, His burial in a rich man's tomb, and His resurrection, our Lord Jesus is fully identified as the Christ of prophecy.

Third, the writers of the gospels and epistles contained in the New Testament believed, without hesitation or question, in the inspiration of the prophets and the divine truthfulness of what they had spoken. They also believed that Jesus of Nazareth was the Christ spoken of by the prophets, and that in every essential particular He fulfilled all that they had said and written of Him. We have here three witnesses of highest possible character and trustworthiness to the inspiration and infallibility of the Word of God in this perfect agreement of prophet, Christ, and apostles, all uniting in beautiful harmony around the iden-

TO CALVARY 137

tity and Deity of our crucified and risen Lord.

There is no more interesting or profitable study than to take the Old Testament writings concerning the coming, the life, the sufferings, and the final victory and glory of our Lord Jesus, and then to turn to the New Testament and, following the footsteps of the earthly life and ministry of our Lord, to notice how perfectly that life, with its sorrows and its blessings upon men, fits into the prediction contained in the prophecies of the Old Testament. There is no possible way to account for this perfect harmony and agreement except we acknowledge at once that the ancient prophets were inspired and that Christ is divine.

Much prophecy has no direct reference to Christ. We find many prophecies concerning the growth, development, and prosperity of Israel. Here their backslidings are foretold, the fall of Jerusalem and the dispersion of the Jews are faithfully pointed out; their sufferings, wanderings, and scatterings through all the nations of the earth are foreseen, and their final restoration is promised. We also have prophecies concerning the fate that was to overtake great heathen cities and the punishment that would fall upon those nations who persecuted the Jews.

The devout student of prophecy will only be able to rightly divide the word of truth when he recognizes the fact that one group of prophecies concerning Christ points to His first coming in humiliation to suffer for a lost race, and to set on foot a scheme of redemption and a gospel evangel to bring the race to repentance and saving faith; and that another group of prophecies points to His second coming in power and great glory to reign and rule over a redeemed people. In the first coming of our Lord those splendid prophecies of His lordship, reign and rule as King of kings and Lord of lords were not fulfilled; but the prophecies concerning His humiliation and suffering were so completely fulfilled in every detail we need have no uneasiness with reference to those inspired promises which point to His coming in power and glory. The fulfillment of the prophecies concerning His humiliation, His sufferings and death have been so accurate in every detail that they offer a firm foundation upon which to rest our faith that the day of His second coming, glory, and victorious reign will dawn with triumph. The Word of God, through His inspired seers, has not failed and cannot fail.

The text refers to a conversation which took place between Jesus and two of His disciples directly after His resurrection, as they walked together up the road from Jerusalem to Emmaus. The disciples were lamenting the death of their Lord, and were quite puzzled over some rumors they had heard with reference to His resurrection. Believing Jesus to be a stranger in the community they undertook to give Him some outline of the sad events which had occurred during the past few days. As Jesus saw how utterly they failed to comprehend Him and His mission He rebuked them for their "slowness of heart to believe all that the prophets had spoken. And beginning at Moses and all the prophets, he expounded unto them in all the scriptures the things concerning himself."

If in the conversation the disciples had referred to the cruelties heaped upon Jesus by those who crucified Him He could have quoted to them from the 22nd Psalm: "All they that see me laugh me to scorn: they shoot out the lip, they shake the head, saying, He trusted on the Lord that he would deliver him: let him deliver him, seeing he delighteth in him." He also might have mentioned to them in the same Psalm, "They part my garments among them, and cast lots upon my vesture." He perhaps reminded them of a prophecy in Zech. 11:12, "And I said unto them, If ye think good, give me my price; and if not, forbear. So they weighed for my price thirty pieces of silver. And the Lord said unto me, Cast it unto the potter: a goodly price that I was priced at of them. And I took the thirty pieces of silver, and cast them to the potter in the house of the Lord."

Our Lord must have called their attention to that beautiful prophecy in Micah 5: "But thou, Bethlehem Ephratah, though thou be little among the thousands of Judah, yet out of thee shall he come forth unto me that is to be ruler in Israel: whose goings forth have been from of old, from everlasting." He could hardly have omitted calling their attention to Isaiah 53, which so vividly describes His humble person, patient sufferings, and His cruel death. "He was despised and rejected of men; a man of sorrows, and acquainted with grief: and we hid as it were our faces from him."

And so Isaiah goes forward centuries before the birth of Christ, giving in minute detail the incidents connected with His sufferings and death for the sins of the race.

Our Lord may have quoted from Isaiah 7:14: "Therefore the Lord himself shall give you a sign; Behold a virgin shall conceive, and bear a son, and shall call his name Immanuel." With reference to His resurrection He could have pointed them to that Psalm in which it is said, "For thou wilt not leave my soul in the grave, neither wilt thou suffer thine Holy One to see corruption." He could have referred them to the fact that way back in Psalm 22, the prophet poet of Israel had written the very words of His lamentation on the cross, "My God, my God, why hast thou forsaken me?" He could have pointed out in Zech. 9, a prophecy that they themselves had seen fufilled, when He rode into Jerusalem, which was written centuries before His birth: "Rejoice greatly, O daughter of Zion; shout, O daughter of Jerusalem: behold thy King cometh unto thee; he is just, and having salvation; lowly, and riding upon an ass, and upon a colt the foal of an ass."

TO CALVARY

In Exodus 12:46, the Hebrews were instructed that no bone of the passover lamb should be broken. David, referring to the Christ, says: "He keepeth all his bones: not one of them is broken." Turning to John 19:33, we read, "Then came the soldiers, and brake the legs of the first, and of the other which was crucified with him. But when they came to Jesus, and saw that he was dead already, they brake not his legs. But one of the soldiers with a spear pierced his side, and forthwith came there out blood and water. And he that saw it bare record, and his record is true; and he knoweth that he saith true, that ye might believe. For these things were done, that the scripture should be fulfilled, A bone of him shall not be broken." It is also said by the Psalmist, "They looked on him whom they pierced."

We readily recall the fact that when our Lord was found to be dead and the soldiers refrained from breaking His legs, they made sure of His death by driving a spear into His side and gazing upon Him as the blood and water trickled from His wound.

What a complete and perfect foundation the Old Testament Scriptures offer for the entire superstructure of the New Testament Scriptures, the Messiahship of Jesus Christ, His Godhead, the Christian Church, world evangelism, and the blessed hope of His second coming in glory and power to bring order out of chaos, peace out of war, plenty out of want, restful faith out of all doubts, and complete satisfaction to all the hunger and longing of the human soul.

The Old Testament and the New are united in perfect and beautiful harmony, bound together inseparably in the life, the love, the death, and resurrection of our Lord Jesus. We rest our faith and peacefully trust the salvation of our immortal souls upon the truth of these scriptures, the identity of the Messiah, His deity and eternal Godhead, His power to save from sin, to sanctify our souls, and present us without spot or wrinkle to His Father in the presence of the holy hosts of heaven.

The Lord Jesus Christ in Old Testament and New is the answer of God to the deep longings of the human soul. The spirit of man created in the image and likeness of its Maker, cannot, will not, be content or satisfied with material things. It has appetites that cannot be satisfied with the things of time; it has a thirst that cannot be slaked with all the waters of Niagara; a hunger that cannot be fed by the cattle upon a thousand hills. Wealth only increases its inertia and dissatisfaction. The things of this world, at their full, only remind us of its starving emptiness. The immortal soul of man has a hungering and thirsting that nothing in all the universe can feed and quench but God Himself.

Man was created for God, and God has mercifully implanted in him a cry that can only be hushed when the wandering child feels the embrace of the infinite arms of the eternal Father; a loneliness that can but long for the bread at the Father's house; a desolation that cannot find peace and rest until it finds it in companionship with Jesus. Jesus Christ is all and in all. Jesus Christ found, trusted in, realized in the forgiveness of sins, in the cleansing of the heart from all moral depravity and corruption, in the outpouring of His infinite love, is heaven. He is eternal life. To believe in Him in the fullness of His grace and power, and to rest one's trust in Him, is to have entered upon eternal life here without any fears or misgivings with regard to the hereafter.

Eternity will be too short to tell our love and ascribe our praise for thee! Thou wast with the Father before the world was. Thy coming into the world was not the beginning of thy existence. Thou didst never know sin; temptations were ever hurled at thee in vain. In the glory of thy Godhead thou didst understand Satan and all of his wiles and was infinitely beyond his reach. Thou didst live in the midst of poverty and taste the sorrows of the poor. Thou didst walk and labor with the ignorant and pity their stupidity. Thou didst receive sinners, eat with them, and look with compassion upon their wickedness. Thou didst weep with sorrowing men, and forgive the sinful, but thou wast God, eternal, pre-existent. Thou wast present when the morning stars sang together, and the sons of God shouted for joy. Thout art the same, yesterday, today, and forever. Thou wilt come again. We wait for thee. Years cannot wear out our patience, centuries hinder our longing, or millenniums dim our hope, or hush the joyful song in our souls, as we contemplate thy coming in thy glory, when we shall behold thee King of kings and Lord of lords, and with prophet, priest, apostles and the saints of the ages worship thee in the full content of our raptured and immortal spirits through all eternity. Amen.

CHAPTER XVII

NATIONAL SECURITY

Text: *"Keep and seek for all the commandments of the Lord your God; that ye may possess this good land, and leave it for an inheritance for your children after you forever."* 1 Chron. 28:8.

We have here King David's parting exhortation to Israel. To seek and keep the commandments of God with careful faithfulness was their title deed to the goodly land which had been given; not only for themselves, but also for their children and succeeding generations. To violate God's law was not only to forfeit His blessings but was to rob their posterity of the blessing God purposed to hand down to them; but these blessings were to be passed on to the coming generations through an obedient and faithful people.

The history of Israel demonstrates the fact that to violate the divine law is to forfeit the divine blessing, and invite a visitation of divine judgments. There are no more startling and surprising chapters in all the pages of ancient history than those which record the backsliding and apostasy of Israel and the severity of the judgments which fell upon them. While they were obedient to God they were invincible; God was in their midst, their armies were victorious, their kings were wise, their prophets and priests were holy and the surrounding nations feared, revered and sought commerce with them and wisdom from them. When they forsook the Lord God their kings were profligates, their priests became idolaters, their prophets were slain, their armies were conquered, their commerce perished, and their pagan foes triumphed over them. The beautiful city of Jerusalem was sacked and burned; their people were carried into captivity and scattered throughout the world a living witness to the inspiration of their prophets who warned them against sin and predicted the calamities and captivities that would be visited upon them. The bleak mountains and barren hills of Palestine have stood through the centuries like tombstones over the graves of a dead and ruined nation, solemn and majestic testimonials to the fact that, however great and favored a people may be, when they violate and trample under foot God's commandments they may be sure that their sins will find them out, and His judgments will be visited upon them.

Not only the Word of God speaks plainly but the voice of history speaks positively in harmony with the Word of God. Sin brings suffering, sorrow and ruin. God has not changed; nations that sin against Him court and invite waste, war, fire, bloodshed, the burden of taxes, the breaking down of the moral barriers, the destruction of reverence for God, divine and civil law, respect for womanhood, the sacredness of the home, and all that makes for the happiness of humankind.

God has chosen and prepared Canaan land for a chosen and prepared people. He made it to flow with milk and honey. It was a goodly land; it was centrally located so that its life, its teachings, its Holy Scriptures, its devout priests, its great prophets, would powerfully influence the nations round about. In the plan of God Israel was to be salt and light to the surrounding nations. While she kept the covenant of God, obeyed and served in reverence and holy fear she wielded so powerful an influence that people came from afar to look upon her glory, listen to her wisdom, and carry back to their people the profound impressions made upon them, and the story of a great prosperous nation whose Lord was the God of the universe, the Maker and Ruler of all things.

There is no way to calculate the untold benefits, the powerful uplifting influences that Israel would have wielded upon the pagan nations had she remained true to God and His laws, and let Him lead her forth from one crowning victory to another, with wave after wave of prosperity and blessing, filling her with divine fulness and overflowing, to bless the nations of the earth. But alas, she sinned. She trampled upon the divine law. She violated her holy covenant with God. She fell into ruin and desolation and the nations whom she should have blessed looked with derision and contempt upon her ruins, rejected and blasphemed the God against whom she had so grievously sinned.

Sin has a wide, almost an endless, influence for the preventing of that which is good, and the promotion of that which is evil. Once committed, it goes on in its blighting influence through the family, the community, the nation, the world, and out into eternity with its burden of wrecked and ruined humanity. Israel not only sinned against God, she sinned against herself, her children, her posterity for thousands of years to come, the nations surrounding her, and the whole human race. Her sin, with its fearful consequences, has gone on through the centuries, and will carry its sad wail of sorrow throughout the lengthening years of eternity.

Let us look for something like a parellel of Israel in modern times. Take our own nation. What a marvelous country! God created and kept it here through the centuries. He hid in its bosom stores of untold wealth in coal, oil, iron, copper, silver and gold. He grew upon its surface the greatest forests that ever waved their plumage in praises toward heaven. He spread out its vast plains and enriched them through the decaying vegetation through thousands of years. He covered it with herds of animals suitable for the feeding of mankind. It was luxuriant with wild fruits that grew in bountiful abundance. God was preparing for a great civilization. He wanted a country free from popes and kings with an open Bible and an evangelical religion where the incense of prayer would rise from countless thousands of family altars. He must guard against a domineering, political, dictatorial, ecclesiasticism by permitting many denominations of Protestant Christians to spring up with a close kinship of faith and practice that centered belief in the inspired Scriptures, the virgin birth and deity of Christ, the atonement He made for sin, the new birth by the operation of the Holy Ghost, and a life in harmony with the teachings of the Word of God.

The growth and prosperity of this nation form a new and marvelous chapter in the history of human progress and civilization. The development of this country in a century and a half would seem impossible if it did not stand an assured fact before us. The clearing of the land, the building of great cities, of thousands of miles of railroad, the erection of countless factories, of churches, schools, hospitals, orphanages, homes for the poor and the aged, the palaces of the rich, the good homes of the middle class, the comfortable cottages of the poor, institutions of every kind for the care of the weak, the healing of the sick, the protection and uplift of the feeble and dependent, the discoveries of science, the prolonging of the average of human life, the opening of God's great cupboard of bounties and blessings have far surpassed anything in the history of the past. This country has become a dominant factor in war, in peace, in finance, in commerce, in charities, reaching into untold millions, in missionary enterprises, in Red Cross efforts for the amelioration of human suffering.

Meanwhile, under the blessing of God, we have had a great Bible-reading people. We have been blessed with a number of evangelical Christian organizations that have carried forward revivals, brought millions of people into the churches and no doubt, vast multitudes into the kingdom of God. It is impossible to enumerate the blessings that have come to our nation and gone out into the nations of the world because of the gospel preached and the spiritual influences set going, and the good that has come to us of every kind on account of the faith, devotion and evangelical spirit of the Protestant churches of the United States. God has planted us in the midst of the nations, secured our safety surrounding us with boundless seas and frozen zones. We are here for a great purpose. No doubt He has chosen us to give the whole Bible to the whole world, with its Christ who, by the grace of God, hath tasted death for every man, and whose blood cleanseth from all sin.

Behold, in the midst of countless blessings of a growth and prosperity unknown in history, we have come upon evil times. Our schools are becoming hotbeds of infidelity. Thousands of the ministry are giving an uncertain sound with regard to the inspiration of the Scriptures, the deity and atoning merit of our Lord Jesus. Our public schools are teaching the theories of unproven science which is destroying evangelical faith in the minds and hearts of the rising generations. We are becoming a nation of Sabbath breakers. Sunday baseball alone gathers hundreds of thousands of our fellow-citizens in the villages, towns and cities into yelling mobs every Sabbath afternoon at the baseball parks. The moving pictures with scenes of robbery, banditry, illicit love, and vulgarity of every kind, through the days and nights, the Sabbath not excepted, great schools of vice, go on unrestrained, year in and year out. In every seven marriages there is one divorce, homes are broken up, parents are estranged, children are left without guidance or the influence of a happy, consecrated home. Divorced people remarry with utter indifference to the teachings of our Lord, and adultery abounds on every hand. There is an unblushing immodesty among many women, old and young. Men believing themselves to be developed from animals are covetous, lewd, and blasphemous. Politicians are self-seeking and cowardly. Often the courts seem to favor criminals. All over the land officials seem to be in collusion with criminals. Combinations of lawbreakers unite and build up great organizations where they gather in millions of dollars in defiance of law and order. Sympathizers who have grown rich out of the liquor traffic are appointed to enforce prohibition laws. The common industries of labor go on unrebuked all about the land on the Sabbath. Churches are almost empty on

Sabbath evening, streets and parks of the cities are crowded with godless pleasure seekers, multitudes of them, members of the various churches, with a shallow pretext of Christianity. Can a just God look upon these things with indifference? They bring inevitable ruin. If God simply withdraws Himself and leaves these violators of His law alone, they plunge inevitably to destruction. But they drag their posterity with them. They pollute the whole land, they poison the schools of all moral and spiritual life for centuries to come; they entail the blight of their sins upon their children and children's children. The judgments of God are far better than to be forsaken of Him. It is better to have His chastisements than that He should simply leave us to ourselves.

There are dark clouds upon the horizon; there is something strange and sinister in the atmosphere. In the distance there is the rumbling of the wheels of the chariot of the great Judge who is rising up to vindicate Himself and His laws. The people of these United States must seek and keep the laws of God if they would possess this good land, and leave it for an inheritance to their children after them. Keeping His laws we shall enjoy His blessing. Trampling upon His commandments, His judgments are inevitable. This must be true. God cannot be indifferent to the laws He has promulgated for the happiness and welfare of mankind. There are no tyrannies in the divine laws; they are legislated in wisdom and mercy; obedience to them will secure the highest good; violation of them will inevitably bring destruction.

CHAPTER XVIII

(We are letting this sermon come last in this book of sermons, because it was the last sermon preached by Dr. Morrison at Elizabethton, Tenn., where he died March 24, 1942.)

HOW TO BRING A SINNER TO CHRIST

Text: *"When Jesus saw their faith, he said unto the sick of the palsy, Son, thy sins be forgiven thee."* Mark 2:5.

The account of the healing of the paralytic as given in the Gospel by Mark is one of the most interesting of all the miracles performed by our Lord. In this, we find not only the healing of the body, but the forgiveness of sin; and we judge that this was true in every case that the faith that enabled Jesus to heal also enabled Him to forgive. There never was or is any question in the mind of the faithful about His power, both to heal the sick and forgive the sinful. Unbelief is the only obstacle that stands in the way of the mighty works of Christ.

There is a very interesting human element in the account, as Mark gives it to us, which is most suggestive. It was quite fortunate for this paralytic that he had four friends who had great faith in Jesus. His condition was such that he needed a group of believers to lay hold upon his cot and bring him into the presence of Christ. He was helpless; without some human assistance he

TO CALVARY

would have undoubtedly died of palsy in his sin, but there were four men who believed that Jesus was more than master of the situation.

These men were also concerned for their brother. They would not be content to let him remain sick and helpless when Jesus was so able to heal, and within reach of their helpless friend. Their faith in Christ, and their love for their neighbor set them going. They went after him; they assured him of both the power and the disposition of Jesus, the compassionate and mighty Healer of the sick. He was no doubt thoroughly convinced and thankful for assistance.

This faith in Christ and love for the neighbor united the four men in zealous effort. I imagine that I can see them hurrying away to the home of their sick friend; they are walking rapidly. they are close together, and are conversing with eagerness among themselves. They break in upon their friend with enthusiasm surprising him with good news; they are all about his bed, all speaking at once and confirming each other's testimony. He is convinced; their enthusiasm and faith are communicated to him, and at once each man seizes a corner of the sick man's couch and they are away to the Lord. I judge there is no debate, one insisting that they carry him through the field, another contending for a back alley, another for Broadway, and another for Main Street. Faith and love, along with enthusiastic service, are very unifying. They at once agree upon the shortest and quickest route to bring their needy brother into the presence of the Master.

At one time, their way seemed blocked, but it is difficult to block the way of earnest men full of faith and on fire with love. The house is crowded, the doors are full, the windows are jammed. They possibly hesitate for a moment with no thought of giving up their object and at once they decide to climb up on top of the house. You understand that these oriental houses were flat-roofed, and that there were outside stairways leading to the top of the house which was a comfortable place for rest in the cool breeze after the setting of the sun. These men betake themselves to this stairway and are soon upon the roof, locating the Lord beneath them. At once they begin tearing off the roof; directly there is an opening; and with cords they lower the sick man down upon the very heads of the throng, who in astonishment press out of the way, and the sick man on his cot is stretched out at the feet of Jesus. How fortunate for this poor fellow that he had friends who were determined, who would overcome obstacles, who would rip the roof off a house but what they would bring a helpless brother to the feet of the Master.

Jesus looks up to see where the man came from and there are four heads filling the hole through which the sick man descended. They are looking straight into the face of Jesus. Faith is written all over their faces. Every lineament beams with confidence. Their eyes are full of trust. It isn't necessary for them to speak; Jesus can see their faith. While their lips utter no sentences, their faith speaks in eloquence. It says, "Master, we know who you are; we believe in your power, your compassion, your love; we know that you can heal this man, and we believe you will. We have brought him to you for that purpose; our efforts are ended; here thy power begins."

Jesus could not disappoint these men. It was not in His infinite heart to do so. He never did such a thing before nor since through all the centuries; faith appeals to Him, moves Him, and secures from Him the expression of His love and blessing of His power.

Jesus says, "Son, thy sins be forgiven thee." This was a surprise. At once, it awakens criticism; complaint is raised in the company. Some one who has no faith, no love, has brought no needy person, torn up no roof, at once says, "Who can forgive sins but God only?" Jesus rebuked him and said, "Whether it is easier to say to the sick of the palsy, Thy sins be forgiven thee; or to say, Arise, and take up thy bed, and walk?" Jesus was manifesting His absolute authority, His Godhead, His rulership over disease and sin, and He continued: "But that you may know that the Son of man hath power on earth to forgive sins, (he saith to the sick of the palsy,) I say unto thee, Arise, and take up thy bed, and go thy way into thine house."

The man was healed and forgiven. He leaped up and seized his cot. It was not necessary to crawl out through the hole in the roof; the people gave way and let him walk out at the door.

We have here a wonderful lesson on *how to bring men to Christ*. First of all, the sinner is a spiritual paralytic. He will not get to the Lord by himself. He needs help, must have help. Revivals do not start themselves. Sinners do not stumble about in their spiritual blindness and accidentally run up on Jesus. It was the plan of God to use men to win men. He appoints His children to go and bring the lost to Him. In order to have a revival of religion and the winning of souls there must be faith in Jesus Christ, faith in His Deity, His Godhead, His authority and power to forgive sins, and His willingness to do it. There must be faith that He can and will save, not only the children, the decent people, the young folks, but that His power can reach those in the far country who have been smitten by sin, who are paralyzed in wickedness, who are dead in trespasses, who are far away. There must be a faith that claims the worst of sinners.

This faith must have for its companion and yokefellow, love. There must be Christian love for the worst of men. There must be a holy longing that goes out for the outcast, the drunkard, the thief, the criminal, the vilest of women, and those prodigals who have wandered farthest from the Father's House. This faith and love must be united and produce service. There must be action; an inactive faith and a timid love that hesitate to put forth effort are of little worth. Faith, love, effort, combination, zeal that will not hesitate, that will not be blocked nor halted; that will climb up on housetops, tear up roofs, invent means and find out ways to bring men to Christ,— these are what count, that bring revivals, that rescue the perishing, that rob Satan of his victims led at his will; that glorify God, that give Jesus an opportunity to show what He can do.

Observe that this man got more than he was expecting; more than his friends were looking for. They sought to get him healed, but he received the forgiveness of his sins. How like our Lord! There is more in Him than we know. He gives greater blessing than we are expecting. He pours out grace and mercy abundantly, if we lay our desires at His feet and lift to Him our faces radiant with faith. I have no doubt this man, once helpless with palsy and lost in sin, is somewhere today in the grand galleries of the universe with our Lord. Those four men with faith and love for capital to begin business with started things going that will go through all eternity.

Let the children of God get busy; kindle the fires of your faith; warm up your heart with love; locate the helpless; find out where the sinners are; go after them; bunch together; search them out; impart your enthusiasm to the dull, dead souls of the lost; arouse them; bring them in; overcome the obstacles; break the fence down; tear the roof off; press through the throng; let nothing prevent; God delights in a holy recklessness that will not be stopped by any obstacle. "The kingdom of heaven suffereth violence, and the violent take it by force."

There is no work so great and blessed, and such a means of grace to the worker, as bringing souls to Christ. If you have faith, and love, and religious industry, and holy zeal, you can bring a soul to Jesus; then you have accomplished a greater work than to lead an army to victory, to build a city, or to rule an empire.

www.ingramcontent.com/pod-product-compliance
Lightning Source LLC
Chambersburg PA
CBHW031355040426
42444CB00005B/296